THE
STRATEGIC
STUDENT
VETERAN

Successfully Transitioning from the
Military to College Academics

THE STRATEGIC STUDENT VETERAN

Successfully Transitioning from the
Military to College Academics

DAVID CASS

Uvize Inc. • *Boulder, Colrado*

Publisher: Uvize Inc. Editor: Jody Berman
Cover and Book Design:

ISBN: 1499341245
ISBN 13: 9781499341249

Uvize Inc. *www.uvize.com*

This book is dedicated to

all those who served in the Armed

Forces of the United States and their families

Contents

Introduction

A human being is not attaining his
full heights until he is educated.
—Horace Mann

According to Student Veterans of America (SVA), approximate-ly half of student veterans will not graduate in six years. Eighty-five percent of student veterans are over the age of twenty-four, and almost half have a family to care for. Most veterans have en-dured multiple extended wartime deployments, and reservists are often mobilized to active duty during the course of their educa-tion. Furthermore, student veterans haven't been in the academic environment for many years. Taking all this into consideration, I can certainly understand why student veteran graduation rates trail those of traditional students. While student veterans bring great strengths to college campuses, the transition to college can be very difficult and too often leads to attrition. Graduation rates are widely debated, but here is one thing that we can all agree on: the graduation rate among our nation's veterans is *unsatisfactory*, needs to improve, and can improve.

Literally, billions of dollars are lost annually on college attri-tion and wasted GI Bill benefits. Such staggering figures do not even begin to address the number of students simply underachiev-ing (e.g., B students who could be A students). For veterans, the transition to college academics can be a difficult one for two major reasons. First, veterans are moving from a very structured environment to an extremely unstructured environment. Second, veterans are moving from a very team-centric culture to a very self-centered culture. These two factors can unnecessarily make a veteran feel like a fish out of water, and too often, it's enough to defeat the student. Veterans are smart and mature, but waiting until arrival on campus to figure out academics is a dire mistake—victory takes place before the battle in the preparation. The mission of *The Strategic Student Veteran* is to teach veterans how to navigate and succeed in the college academic environment. While the life transition for veterans goes far beyond academics, by lessening the stress of the academic transition, the likelihood of success is significantly increased. One goal of this book is to help raise graduation rates among our nation's veterans. A second and larger goal is to help students efficiently navigate their college career and raise their GPAs to ultimately improve their career opportunities.

Why do so many students struggle during their first year in college? The main reason is their inability to effectively transition from high school or the military to college academics—yet this struggle has little to do with one's level of intelligence; it has everything to do with the lack of education on this transitional period. The bright side is that failure is preventable and success in the form of a high grade point average (GPA) is achievable for almost every student regardless of his or her natural aptitude or academic background.

The Strategic Student Veteran is your roadmap for demystifying college academics and creating a strategic mind-set for academic success. It is an outgrowth of lessons learned from three key experiences in my life and career:

1. my freshman year at Tulane University achieving mediocre results,
2. my experience as a freshmen academic advisor and adjunct professor at the University of Colorado at Boulder, and
3. my return to college at age thirty-three to retake freshmen-level classes while applying the strategies in this book and interviewing many student veterans in the process

I spent almost four years interviewing college freshmen about their academic habits as an NROTC professor before I went back to school to test the strategies I collected. I wanted to retake classes I took over a decade earlier, take some new classes, and put into practice what I had learned from my students. Essentially, I joined individuals like you who will benefit from this book. The results were amazing: my ability to learn with a new mind-set and strategy dramatically changed for the better.

Ideally, this book should be read before you enter college, though any college student who wants to improve his or her transition to college academics will glean valuable information from it.

How This Book Will Help You

The Strategic Student Veteran provides proven, realistic methods to implement in your academic life. Specifically, it will:

- teach you how to develop a mind-set that was not necessary in high school or in the military
- show you ways to accept control and ownership of your education
- help you efficiently manage your time
- guide you in creating a plan for your academic career (no, your school will not do this for you!)

In other words, you'll learn how to incorporate academic structure into a very unstructured system.

This book also advises on what not to do. A major benefit of knowing what not to do is that it helps you recognize inefficient behaviors that will undoubtedly surround you. Being able to identify those behaviors is the first and most important step in avoidance. If you take nothing else from this book but the ability to identify and avoid adopting the inefficient patterns you see in others, you're already way ahead of the game. Therefore, I will discuss poor habits almost as much as good habits.

The Strategic Student Veteran is divided into three parts. Part 1 describes how and why this book came to be and why developing self-reliance and managing your GPA are critical to your college success. Part 2 discusses the necessary academic skills you'll need and teaches you how to apply them. Part 3 discusses dealing with stress and understanding the role of technology in education.

Who Will Benefit from This Book?

The Strategic Student Veteran is designed for active-duty armed forces members or veterans who are either just about to enter college or are early in their college career. Additionally, educators, coaches, and advisors who are concerned about their students and want to help them succeed will find the tools in this book invaluable.

This Book Is Different from Other Books

The Strategic Student Veteran is *not* a magic formula resulting in straight A's. Any book claiming to have a single system that helps all students achieve college success is making a false claim. There are many study strategies in book stores; some will work for you, and some will not. Although this book does cover essential study techniques, its main purpose is to help you transition your mindset and manage resources such as time (chapter 4). Finally, this book is not about shortcuts and it's not for students who aren't ready and willing to work.

My main criticism of some of the "Get an A" books out there is that the author spent his or her time only interviewing professors, straight-A students, and Ivy Leaguers. They never interviewed the students who struggle to discover what *not to do*. Learning what not to do is half the battle! While I have tremendous respect for Ivy League students (most of them anyway), the fact is they've probably always been great students (that's why they are where they are). Ivy League students don't know what it's like not to "get it," and therefore, their lessons are incomplete. A complete library of lessons includes those learned from students who have experienced academic struggles and subsequently succeeded.

The best lessons in this book are derived from my D or C students, who, through strategic changes, learned to become B or A students. The best lessons are also from below-average high school students who went on to become great college students, students who went to college, left, joined the military, and came back to succeed. These students truly know about strategizing and maximizing potential. I was shocked to find other authors have ignored this population in their research.

As a college freshman advisor, I was unable to find a book that supplied what my struggling students needed in order to adapt to the challenges of college academics. Moreover, these students needed to hear about other struggling students who are now successful. This book is a result of collecting their input, developing various learning strategies, and testing these theories firsthand when I returned to college as a freshman. I routinely get asked why I returned to school to take undergraduate classes, and my answer is simple, "to test academic strategies and deliver only the most effective ones." Any author who hasn't actually tested the strategies that they write about is delivering hearsay. Would a chef serve a meal without first tasting it?

Forget your high school experiences in academics and throw away your SAT/ACT scores; none of it is a predictor of your future collegiate success. Your military experience will help you succeed but only if properly harnessed. Regardless of your military rank, you had a schedule and orders to follow; now you are the one who will create your own schedule and issue your own orders. As you read this book, think about shifting your mind-set to one of a strategic student. Once you've shifted your mind-set to a strategic one, you will truly be amazed at your capacity to learn and ultimately get great grades. I was amazed at my ability to apply these strategies, and I know, with 100 percent certainty, that I did *not* get smarter over the past fifteen years. College will move fast, and a damaged semester is very difficult to undo. So read on, and start maximizing your learning potential and attaining your desired GPA.

The Academic Cockpit

My students will tell you I'm a sucker for metaphors. As a former US Navy pilot, I tell my students that they need to climb into their academic cockpit in order to take control of their academics.

When a pilot climbs into an aircraft, he or she takes complete control of that machine. The aircraft will do exactly what you tell it to do or let it do. If you let it fly into a mountain, it will do it without asking any questions. If the pilot doesn't fly the plane, the plane will fly the pilot; the latter scenario never ends well. A student needs to think of a semester the same way. Fly your GPA, or it will fly you…straight down.

Anyone who has seen the gauges in a cockpit may think it looks quite complicated. Actually, those gauges just represent feedback—feedback from the airplane telling the pilot one of two things: *direction or performance.* Students need to consider these two themes every day if they want to stay competitive. Am I on course? How am I performing?

Here is one of the crucial mistakes most college students make: *they use their grades as the sole measurement of direction and performance.* Grades are the results of past performance (what you did before test day) and therefore are not an effective data point for planning. Ask a student how she's doing in a class, and she'll likely reference a recent test or paper score.

I understand the confusion over why grades are a poor indicator of performance when planning academic strategy, which is why I want to stick with the cockpit metaphor. What if there was a caution light in a cockpit to alert the pilot that "You just crashed"— a big, blinking red light telling you that you just flew into the ground? It's a little late for that info, isn't it? When a student finds out at midterms that he is not performing well, it is also a bit late. Now he is fighting for a B or C instead of an A. And the fight just got a lot harder because the stuff that he just did not learn so well is going to be on the final—not quite as dire as an aircraft crash but the point is the damage has already been done.

An A is a grade with very little room for damage; therefore, a student should approach a semester with a damage-control mind-set. A cockpit tells a pilot if there is a problem developing before she crashes. A student needs to monitor his or her performance before being graded. Once students make the revelation that grades are an end point and the real performance is what they do between tests; they become different students. They simply need a system to self-monitor direction and performance. *The Strategic Student Veteran* will teach students how to self-monitor. Good luck on your transition to becoming a strategic student. I am confident this book will help you to reach your academic goals.

PART ONE

Applying the Strategic Student Mind-Set

Chapter 1

Preventing Academic Problems: Developing the Strategic Student Mind-Set

However beautiful the strategy, you should
occasionally look at the results.
—Winston Churchill

During my first year as an NROTC professor and academic advisor, I found myself saying to students, "If I knew then what I know now, I would have been a straight-A student." I realized one day that this claim did not provide students with any tangible strategies to utilize in their studies. Furthermore, I recognized that I couldn't even validate this claim, so I decided to go seek evidence. I set out to prove that better management techniques and a strategic mentality can make you a great student regardless of your natural abilities.

This chapter covers the major periods of my college and academic careers that fueled the writing of *The Strategic Student Veteran*. Understanding the background of this book will help give you confidence in the book's theories and help you implement the strategies in your own career. This chapter will also present reasoning for my return to college and will help you develop *The Strategic Student Veteran* mind-set. If you are not interested in theory, simply skip ahead to the next chapter and learn about the most important quality for academic success: self-reliance.

My Undergraduate Years and Flight School

Like many college students, I arrived at my college campus far from home and didn't have a clue as to what I was embarking upon. When I arrived at Tulane University in New Orleans, I faced many life transitions: leaving home, living independently, developing a new social life, learning to do laundry, and of course studying in a completely different academic environment. Academics became just one thing on a long list of life changes that I was adjusting to. Veterans arriving on campus have certainly adjusted to life away from home; however, the military learning environment is significantly different from the college learning environment.

Academically speaking, I did what I thought was enough. I saw my advisor when I had to, and I studied mostly when I had a test coming up or a project due. In other words, I approached college like the average college student, and my results were also quite average. I graduated college in four years with a bachelor's degree in political science and a 3.2 GPA, though I really struggled with attaining academic focus—and I know now that I underachieved.

Following college, I barely managed to get into the navy's flight school in Pensacola, Florida. When I showed up at flight school, I was quite intimidated by the academic achievements of my new classmates. They were engineers, cum laudes, and students from the Naval Academy and prestigious Ivy League schools, and some had already earned a master's degree. I was a kid who had scraped by in college. I decided there was only one way to succeed and compete with those I perceived to be more intelligent: I had to study smarter and more efficiently than my fellow classmates.

Flight school moved at a furious pace. You studied one day, and you performed what you learned with an instructor the next. Every day was a test, and there was no back of the classroom to hide out in. It was a great educational experience and lesson in consistency in learning. I couldn't believe how much material I could absorb with daily effort and consistent study sessions. I focused a great deal on *how* to study and *how* to approach material. Consistency in education is a theme I would later return to as an academic advisor and professor; it's also a major theme of this book.

My Return to Academia as an Advisor

When I heard that the navy had a program that assigns officers to universities to teach and manage ROTC (Reserve Officers' Training Corps) programs, I actively sought placement. I interviewed at the University of Colorado, Boulder, and was lucky to be hired as an assistant professor of naval science. My title, often called adjunct professor, means the university invited me to teach for three to four years based on my experiences as a naval officer, but I was never on a traditional tenure track. Not being a traditionally trained educator allowed me to view education with a perspective unlike that of a conventional educator and thus produce unconventional strategies.

In addition to managing programs and teaching a naval strategy and history class, I was also given the title freshman academic advisor. My initial impression was that as an advisor, I would mainly remind students to study hard and tell them to work on their time management skills. I couldn't have been more wrong; academic advising became the biggest challenge of my job and a significant focus of my life.

At the end of my first year of teaching and advising, I had two semesters of grades and data to study. The polarization of my students' grades puzzled me. The levels of success varied greatly, and two groups dominated. I had a group of students with great results and a group with lousy results, yet not that many in the middle range (B students). Unfortunately, much like the national trend, a portion of my students did not return to the University of Colorado for their sophomore year. To this day, I feel like I let down my struggling students. I was determined to do better by my next class. Figure 1.1 is a representation of my students' results at the end of freshman year. Two groups should jump out at you. The two tallest peaks are the 1.9 to 2.2 GPA group and the 3.3 to 3.6 GPA group. That means I had many great students *and* many struggling students. In fact, the group that captured the class average of 2.80, which lies somewhere in the middle, comprised only about 13 percent of all my students.

Freshmen GPA Groups

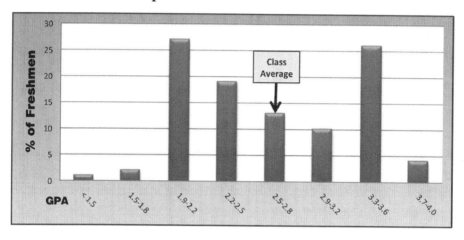

Figure 1.1. At the end of my first year advising, my class average was a 2.80 GPA. The class average often advertised at colleges does not communicate the polarity that may exist in a class.

The "class average" of 2.80 (which is the approximate national average) could give students a false sense of security. *The class average is misleading: there are two distinct groups causing that single data point.* Which group would you want to be in? It is a choice.

My first reaction to the results shown in figure 1.1 was that some students were simply smarter than others. I was very wrong, but if this conclusion were true, I would have seen a normal distribution of GPAs representing the varying levels of intelligence in the population as represented in figure 1.2.

Theoretical Freshmen GPAs

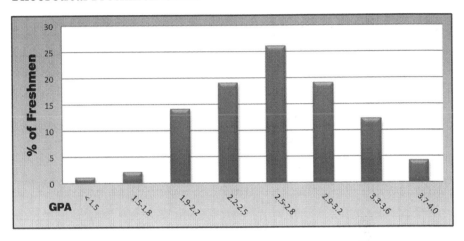

Figure 1.2. If the average GPA meant that most students received at or around that GPA, the distribution of students would look like this (but it doesn't).

Class averages can be misleading (see figure 1.1). Imagine if you had five students, four of them received straight A's, and one student failed every class. The average GPA of this group is 3.20. Did most students receive 3.20? No—that number doesn't represent the group well at all. Look deeper into average GPAs when you see them advertised.

Making Sense of the Successes and Failures of My Freshman Students

I correlated my students' precollege performance with their college grades and found that traditional indicators of intelligence (such as SAT scores) were not strongly correlated with collegiate success or failure. In other words, if you were the smart kid in high school, you wouldn't be an automatic success in college. Contrarily, if you struggled in high school, that wouldn't mean you couldn't be wildly successful in college. I saw both of these scenarios happen many times.

I also determined that a student's gender and academic major were not predictors of whether the student would struggle or be wildly successful. What follows is an overview of the conclusions I derived from analyzing the successes and failures of my students and the many hours of interviews I conducted with them.

Conclusions

There was one dominant common theme among my struggling students: they didn't have a plan or system for managing resources. By resources, I mean time, study plans, and campus support resources. Now, if my struggling students were the ones who didn't have a plan, the successful group was quite the contrary. The successful students were efficient managers of resources. They had a system, and they tracked their progress, though it's important to note that not all of their systems were the same. There is no "right" system. The point is that each successful student had personalized some sort of system that worked for him or her.

Another commonality among my successful students was that they tracked progress by a variable other than grades—usually, they used time. Semesters rarely go exactly according to plan, but the big difference with successful students was that they knew when they were off track and formed a new plan. The struggling students weren't aware they were off track until it was too late.

Designing a Seminar to Help Freshmen Succeed

As a result of the lessons learned, I began designing strategies aimed at preventing academic problems rather than solving them. These strategies would help my students succeed with more self-reliance, and they would certainly make the advisor's job easier. My department's head professor suggested that I put together my results and strategies into a class. Thus, the Introduction to Freshmen Year seminar was born. The class was one day and was followed up with one-on-one advising sessions throughout the year. The class had a very positive response, and I'm proud of the effect it had on my students. The class continued to evolve up until the end of my teaching term, and upon departure, I continued to develop the concepts on which it was based.

Graduate Business School

During my early years as a professor and advisor at the University of Colorado, Boulder, I was also a graduate student. I went to University of Colorado's Leeds School of Business as an evening student and earned a master's degree in business administration. A great entrepreneurship professor at Leeds, Frank Moyes, once said to my business plan class, "A business mind views the world as problems that need to be solved, and entrepreneurs are the ones who seek solutions." At the time, I was seeking a solution to the problem I was seeing among my freshmen students, and an entrepreneurial mind-set helped me analyze the problem.

A business mind-set means that we view the world as constantly seeking balance. In business, we balance risk and rewards. We balance return on investments. We balance data-driven decisions with instinctive decisions. Ultimately, we balance cost and benefits and we even study "balance sheets" in accounting. Business is all about balance and efficiency. Balance is a central theory in business education and a central theory in the strategic student mind-set.

My successful students were efficient managers. They knew how to balance their commitments, their workload, and, most important, their time. My less successful students were always imbalanced, pure and simple. For example, one common trend I saw among low-GPA students is that they often had a high grade in one class. They would even say to me, "But I got an A in (fill in a class name)." My response would be, "That's great, but your GPA is still terrible." A result like this told me they had great potential but were imbalanced in their time allocation. They allocated far too much time (a precious resource) for this one class.

Returning to School as a Freshman

The problem thus far with my academic theories was that I had data from only one group. While I collected many strategies from my freshmen students, I didn't have proof that their success or lack thereof was a direct result of these strategies. I believed it was, but a good academic always seeks proof. Furthermore, I never had a student who implemented *all* of the strategies simultaneously.

Although I learned a great deal about success from my freshmen students, I felt I couldn't truly develop the strategic student concepts unless I lived them. So I made the decision to return to school as a freshman and take freshman-level classes at the University of Colorado, Boulder, and Front Range Community College. I would experiment on myself.

Becoming One of Them

The 1988 movie *Gorillas in the Mist* is based on the best-selling book by scientist Dian Fossey about her studies on African gorillas. How did Dr. Fossey learn so much about gorillas? She joined them. She lived with them; she ate what they ate; she slept where they slept. I am no Dr. Fossey, and I certainly don't want to imply that college freshmen are gorillas, though I do believe the best way to learn about a population is to join them in their natural surroundings. When I would interview college freshmen simply as an advisor, there was always a certain barrier between us. By going back to school and taking a few classes, I could just be one of them and learn the way they were learning. However, unlike Dr. Fossey, I was not willing either to move in with the freshmen or eat what they eat.

The experiment that I was about to launch was a quest to learn and should not be confused with scientific theory and rigorous testing. However, it was extremely important in helping me develop the ideas I learned from my students and also gave me the proof and confidence to be able to tell students, "This stuff works." What follows is an explanation of my experiment with the reasoning and assumptions that helped me draw the conclusions in this book.

The Experiment: Comparing Me and Me

My goal, in the broadest sense, was to assess my ability to learn, study, and take tests after implementing lessons I learned from students during my career as an advisor. I would then compare my results with my results as an eighteen-year-old freshman at Tulane. Because this experiment was not totally scientific, its inherent design is open to valid criticism. Let me address what I think might be the main criticisms.

Criticism: "You can't compare results because you learned much of the material your first time in the class."

Response: I chose classes that I took my freshman and sophomore years over fourteen years prior. I also chose subjects that I haven't studied since then (I could never remember material for that long anyway). I also took a few classes that I hadn't previously taken to simply practice "learning." Learning new material is like painting with a clean palette. I was able to focus on learning and studying but without comparing results.

Criticism: "Class difficulty differs from school to school."

Response: True, to some extent, but there are some subjects where this is minimized. I chose math and science classes only. My reasoning for this is that 100-level science classes are standardized. This means that to be an accredited collegiate science class, every school has to teach the same material. In other words, Chemistry 101 at Harvard teaches the exact same material as Chemistry 101 at a two-year community college in California or at Clemson University in South Carolina and elsewhere.

It's also important to note the time lapse between when I first studied this material and the present has not affected the material. Basic chemistry, physics, statistics, and biology have not changed appreciably, nor will they. More subjective classes like writing or political science would be too difficult to compare because material and grading criteria vary from school to school.

Criticism: "Your lifestyle has changed; how can you compare the two results?"

Response: I agree that my lifestyle has changed. When I was eighteen and a freshman, I did not have a job or any financial responsibilities. In fact, I had all the free time in the world.

When I returned to school at age thirty-two, I had a full-time job (around fifty hours a week), a mortgage, bills, a wife, and a new baby. I couldn't agree more; my lifestyle is certainly different. I was even more disadvantaged in terms of time during my second round.

Criticism: "You took some classes at community college. Those classes are easier."

Response: I did take some classes at a community, or junior, college because I needed to take evening science classes and my local university didn't offer evening sessions. The quality of education at the community college where I took a few classes was just as good and classes were just as difficult as my highly priced university. The professors were exceptional, and many of them previously taught the exact same syllabus at four-year universities. Based on my experience, there is no difference in material or level of difficulty between science classes at a university and a community college.

I do believe the spectrum of student aptitude is wider at a community college. This ranges from brilliant students seeking a cheaper alternative to starting college to high school "screw-ups." Therefore, I did not want to be graded relative to my classmates and I took no classes that were graded on a curve (relative to my classmates). I wanted to be graded on how well I learned the material and nothing else. Therefore, my grades only reflect how I did in terms of learning the material, *not* how I did relative to my classmates.

Further, the only classes I took at the community college were those accepted as credit in the University of Colorado system.

Therefore, they met all university criteria in terms of material covered. I even took state exams when available. For example, in my Chemistry 101 class, I took the American Chemical Society exam, which is the national standard for all university chemistry classes. I did quite well, in fact.

Summary of the Experiment

The results of my "experiment" are more qualitative and, frankly, quite simple: *I learned much better by applying strategic theories.* I absorbed more material more efficiently, and I scored higher grades. My class time was more productive. I never studied more than two hours at a stretch. I never studied late into the night. Keep in mind too that I took these classes at the very busiest time in my life. I was working full-time and had a new baby! My results gave me the confidence to write this book and confidently say: these theories will make you a better student. Before I went back to school, I thought these theories worked; now I know they work.

Classes I Took

The change in grades is not the most important part of my experiment; the changes in my abilities are. But I know my students and readers are curious about my results, so here they are: the before and after.

Class	Before (1994)	After (2009)
Physics I	B-	A
Statistics	N/A*	Pass**
Chemistry I	B-	A
Chemistry II	N/A	A
Biology I	C+	A
Biology II	N/A	A

*N/A indicates I didn't take this class my first time in college.

**Class taken pass/fail because I was a non-degree undergraduate student at University of Colorado, Boulder.

Summary

The material in this book is an aggregation of theories I posited and lessons I learned in college, as a flight student, as an academic advisor and professor, and as a nontraditional student returning to undergraduate studies. This book is about changing your mindset. Some of the strategies will work for you, but some may not. I encourage you to develop strategies of your own or modify those presented here to fit your needs.

The strategic student is a self-reliant student. In the next chapter, you will learn why becoming self-reliant is essential for a smooth and successful transition to college life.

Chapter 2

Transitioning from the Military to College: Becoming a Self-Reliant Student

Education is the most powerful weapon which you can use to change the world.
—Nelson Mandela

Transitioning your mind-set to college academics begins with erasing your framework of the high school academic structure and military education and understanding your new role in the college academic environment. In high school, you may have gotten help (whether you liked it or not) from a teacher, coach, counselor, or parent. In the military, your education was extremely structured and your classmates were on the same schedule. In college, you are in the driver's seat. It's up to you to seek help on your own. Becoming a strategic student means becoming a self-reliant student. This chapter will show you how.

College Academics Versus High School Academics

A general assumption of incoming college freshmen is that college academics are more difficult than high school academics. I don't believe college academics are more difficult—at least at the freshmen level. Yet freshman year is pivotal because this is when you either "figure it out" or become convinced it's "too hard." I personally didn't figure it out my freshman year at Tulane University (or sophomore year…but let's not tug at that string), and that's a main reason why, as a freshman advisor, I wanted to help students make their college transition a more successful one than mine was.

As I mentioned in chapter 1, my first class of advisees (all freshmen) was polarized between success and failure, and I wasn't sure why. There simply weren't many middle-of-the-packers, and I incorrectly assumed that the more intelligent students succeeded and the less intelligent failed. Many struggling students started visiting me, and they all shared something like this, "But I did fine in high school. I guess college is just much more difficult." They too were incorrect. Freshmen college academics are often a review of senior-level high school courses, with a deeper dive as time moves on in the semester. The problem is magnified by your time in the military. Figure 2.1 illustrates how a military training and college day really differs.

Comparison of a Military Day and a College Day

Typical Military Training Day	Typical College Day

• 0700 Muster
• 0730 Physical Training
• 0830 Tactics Class Part I
  1000 Tactics Class Part II
• 1100 Chow
• 1230 Field Training Part I
  1430 Field Training Part II
• 1700 Chow
• 1900 Study Hours
• 2200 Lights out
	• 10:00 a.m. Biology 101
	• 2:00 p.m. European History
	  Yup, that's it.

Notice any difference between the two? Does the college day look much easier? Careful! It's a trap. The problem is not the difficulty of the academic material; it's the educational system you are learning in.

Different Educational System, Different Learning Environment

In high school, classes meet almost every weekday, so even if you aren't studying much at home, there's still a learning opportunity in class daily. And because you turn in so much homework and meet daily, teachers will know quickly if you're falling behind and they'll usually take action to help you. College classes meet at most three times a week. Many meet only twice a week. If you fall behind, no one will know until grades are posted—except for you.

In high school and in the military, there is oversight and guidance almost every step of the way. The bell rings, and you go to class. The bell rings again, and you leave class. You don't even need to think about it. A teacher, coach, or senior ranking figure is almost always kicking your butt. These positive forces don't really exist in college. The class at 10:00 a.m. didn't take attendance. The professor lectures on the subject for those interested in listening, and there's little homework to hand in. *The difference is not the academic material. The difference is the dramatically different learning environment.*

The other major shift that catches students off guard is where the learning takes place. In high school and the military, most of the learning takes place in school. In college, most of the learning takes place outside the classroom (see figure 2.2). I think most students expect this shift but grossly underestimate the degree of the split. I'll elaborate on this concept in chapter 4, but for now, I just want you to grasp how much you are on your own in college. If you start to understand this, you won't be defeated (which happens often) when you arrive on campus. You'll also have a plan, which is exactly what this book is about.

The student who adjusts to this dramatically different environment succeeds. The one who doesn't...well, you know. Understanding this environment change is the basis for your strategic mind-set. Oh, and one other thing: if you are not in class tomorrow at 10:00 a.m., no one will ask why and, to be perfectly blunt, no one will really care that much.

In College, You Trade Classroom Time for Free Time

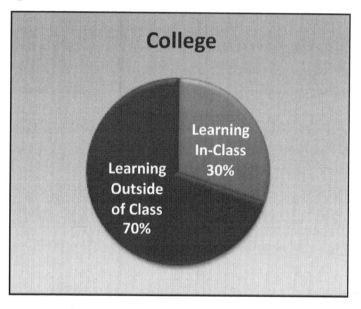

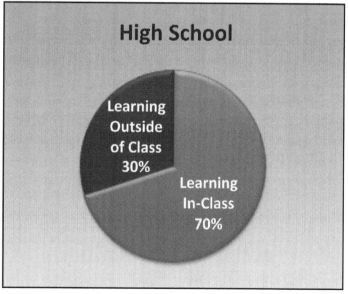

Blink

In his best-selling book *Blink* (2005), Malcolm Gladwell discusses how humans interpret information and make fast decisions based on little real-time information—that is, in a "blink of an eye." It's intriguing how often these snap decisions are correct, even when compared to decisions incorporating great information and deep analysis. As with a seasoned firefighter who senses when a building will collapse seconds before it does, when humans become experienced at something, we become proficient at rapidly predicting the outcome.

As a pilot, I was once told you can't start trusting the hairs on the back of your neck until after you've had at least five hundred hours of flight time. After that many hours of flying, I began to sense how the aircraft was performing and even to sense if something was about to go wrong.

One day, with only about one hundred hours of flight time under my belt, I had just taken off from Naval Air Station Coronado; it was a beautiful San Diego day, and I was enjoying the view of Point Loma. Suddenly, my veteran aircraft commander, Reggie Hammond, grabbed the controls from me, turned the aircraft around, and started heading back toward our base. On the way back, a caution light illuminated, indicating engine trouble. In other words, Reggie knew we had an emergency before the aircraft even knew. How did he know? "I just knew," he said. "Things didn't feel right."

By that point, Reggie had flown about two thousand hours, which helped him make that fast, gut-level decision. Similarly, after a few years of advising freshmen, I developed the ability to predict the needs of my students based on experience.

What Is a Self-Reliant Student?

A self-reliant student is a student who *initiates* action without being prompted by an external source. The external source could be a professor, a parent, an advisor, or maybe a friend. The word *initiate* is key here. Sometimes my students confuse my goal of self-reliance with meaning that I don't want them to need external help or guidance. This is 100 percent *not* what I mean. Every college student will need assistance at some point—that's a normal part of higher education. In college, you can get help if you seek out the proper resource, but you have to initiate the effort.

When I was an advisor, I'd send an e-mail to my students for them to make a midsemester appointment with me to discuss grades. Who do you think were the first ones to respond? You guessed it. Usually my star students were the ones who responded first. The students who needed the appointment least were the first to respond. Coincidence? I doubt it.

Self-Reliance: Predictor of Student Success

Every August, the naval science department at the University of Colorado, Boulder, would host a welcome-to-school orientation for incoming freshmen and their parents. It was always fun. We'd eat burgers, play softball, and provide an opportunity for families to meet our staff. At this event, I was introduced as the freshman advisor for the naval science students. Because dropping a son or daughter off at school, especially if it's far from home, is stressful for parents and students, most students and their families wanted to meet me. The welcome party served to facilitate that, and I was happy to meet my new crop of students. It was during this introduction that a student's likelihood of struggling during their first school year and their potential need for extra attention first surfaced. The introduction process usually went like this: I'd see a student. His or her parents would walk up to me, and all of them would look nervous. One of two things happened next:

1. The *student would introduce* himself and his parents to me.
2. The parents would introduce themselves and the student to me.

After a few years and several welcome orientations later, I concluded that the student who walked up to me and introduced me to her parents was usually proactive. I call her a *driver*. A driver takes control. The student whose parents conducted the introduction was often more dependent on others. I call him *a passenger*. A passenger is along for the ride and doesn't offer much input. Although I couldn't predict the student's academic aptitude or ability from this first impression, I do believe it was telling in terms of which students would be self-reliant and which ones wouldn't be.

The parents who conducted the introduction often proceeded to tell me about their child. I'd sit there and listen while the freshman heard himself being discussed as if he wasn't present. The same parents were often the ones who called me throughout the year to check on their son or daughter. They would often ask me questions they hadn't even asked their student yet, such as, "How is [name] doing?" or "What can she improve on?" I can say this very confidently: the students whose parents called me regularly were almost never academically successful. I discussed this observation with many students, and the conclusion I came to was: students' academic success has little to do with how intelligent they are. It has to do with whether or not they're self-reliant.

Self-reliance is the key ingredient to academic success and the most important quality I saw in my successful students.

They were the same students who made appointments with me regularly without the need for me to send an invitation. They were proactive and didn't wait for guidance to take action. In college, if you wait for guidance to take action, you're going to be too late. While veterans have already left home and generally aren't being guided by parents, I hope you see the point of this story is that as veterans, we were always guided by senior authorities. Losing this level of guidance may seem like no big deal, but to many student veterans, it is.

Let's look at self-reliance in terms of academics. Most schools suggest that a student study two to three hours for every in-class hour. It's a broad rule of thumb. (In chapter 4, I'll discuss the flaws of this rule, but for the sake of discussion, I'll stick with this suggestion to prove a broader point.) Most college classes meet for three hours a week. That means the school recommends you study that subject for six to nine hours a week. Apply this rule to your entire schedule of classes, and 50 to 75 percent of your academic pursuit will take place outside of the classroom. Theoretically, this means that *about 75 percent of your college education is self-guided*!

This point is usually a bit shocking at first, especially to parents. The reason I teach this theme is not to criticize universities. They're doing exactly what they should be doing, and they're doing an excellent job. I teach this to prepare students. They need to know that self-reliance isn't just a nice quality to have; it's absolutely necessary for success. Another reason I teach this is to clarify the role of the student and the role of the university. Once those roles are understood, self-reliance just seems to make more sense to students.

A university's job, in the broadest sense, is research and education. Your college will present you with subject matter—math, science, business, arts, and so on. It will *not* teach you how to study it, which is where you most need learning. Furthermore, your college will *not* teach you time management. Outside of class, you're on your own. There will be academic centers and tutors available if you'd like to use them, but they won't be required. You'll only be required to take a minimum level of credits at school, and the rest is voluntary.

The Self-Reliant Student's Role within the University

It's important to realize that the university's job is to teach subject matter. In class, you will learn some essential points and your professor will present important lessons, but it takes significantly more time outside of class to truly learn the material. So if you understand this point, you're probably one step ahead in realizing that if you're only in class 30 percent of the time, then your university is really only responsible for 30 percent of your education time. You are in charge of the other 70 percent! Imagine if your college websites stated, "We only contribute to 30 percent of your education; the rest is up to you!" This is dramatically different from high school because in high school, bright students can learn most of what they need to know in class. External time is minimal. Parents are often very upset with the college if their son or daughter fails out (I know—I've received that phone call!), but if you understand the role of the student and the school, this misunderstanding won't occur and you can prepare accordingly.

Colleges generally operate in departmental segments. The school of business will largely have no interaction with the school of engineering. Your English professor will probably have no idea what resources are available to help you in your calculus class. Because freshmen often take a wide spectrum of classes to fulfill core requirements, they can be all over campus. Self-reliant students grasp early on that they actually are students at multiple "schools." The larger the campus, the less centralized the resources will be. Each school and department will have separate centers for study rooms, tutors, and so on, so you'll need to seek out the resources within the school/department that houses the class you're taking. It will take a little time and digging to find out what exactly is available, and your professor is a great starting point. Departmental websites also offer lots of information.

I've heard students say on many occasions, "I didn't even know that resource center was there." Remember, no one is going to invite you. You must go on your own. Similarly, a self-reliant student starts a study group and doesn't wait for an invitation to join one. Self-reliance initiates the action, but help is there waiting. Tutors, advisors, study groups, and clubs are all around, but you must contact them yourself.

What to Expect from Your College Advisor

Do you know how many required meetings the average college student has with his or her academic advisor over four years? Two. That's it—one freshman year and one prior to graduation. (Some schools also require an additional meeting if you change majors.)

Advisors are truly there to help, but there's only so much they can do for each student. The very nature of their job imposes limitations that are beyond their control. Once you understand these limitations, you'll learn to better utilize your advisor's services and help him or her to do the job, which is to help you succeed, better! Here are a few of the obstacles an advisor faces:

- **The advisor manages a number of students.**
  At a large university, an academic advisor often has up to five hundred students! This means that during any given semester, you'll likely have only one meeting (at most) and that meeting will be brief. Any other meetings will require an appointment, which may take a few days (or weeks) to schedule. Even at a smaller school, the advisor is greatly limited.
- **There is a time lag before the advisor sees your grades.**
  If you don't access your advisor, the advisor won't know you're having any difficulties until after he or she receives your semester grades. Advisors generally don't see midterm grades, and even if they do, it's still too late for them to do much. Using grades as a performance reference is bit like waiting until you're sunburned to apply sunscreen. The damage is done, and there's not much you can do except plan your next beach day better.
  My point is advisors would rather prevent a problem than try to fix one. Your advisor can't help you repair a broken semester when the semester is already over.
- **Advisors often "ignore" good students.**
  You know the old saying "The squeaky wheel gets the grease." In academia, this statement is too often true. If you're a solid B student (3.0 GPA), you're a very good student. But even though you're a good student, you're striving to be a great student, an A student. You're trying to get into that top law school! You too need assistance getting to the next level, and you have limited time to do it. The problem is your advisor likely will be quite busy with her problematic students.

So, you see, the obstacles are significant, and there's not much advisors can do to eliminate them. My hope is that this book will help you take a more proactive and independent role in your own academic planning. After all, it's your GPA, not your advisor's. You leave school with that GPA, so you have to take ownership of it early on.

Maximizing Your Relationship with Your Advisor

An academic advisor's job at most schools is to provide program guidance. For the most part, your advisor is there for what I call "big picture" items. Such items include:

- degree plans (determining the most effective plan for you to excel and graduate on time)
- program requirements (class and major prerequisites)
- scholarship information
- department and campus resources
- personal crisis (you should alert your advisor if you have a family emergency)
- program changes
- transferability of coursework from different schools
- graduate program advice
- registration information
- career options

To maximize value during your very limited advisor time, you'll need a strategy. For instance, if you have a thirty-minute appointment with your advisor, you do *not* want to spend fifteen minutes discussing something you could have found out on the department's website. Here are three important things you can do to maximize value in those appointments.

1. If your advisor schedules the meeting, have specific questions prepared. Send an e-mail a few days prior asking if there are any items or information he or she would like you to bring.
2. If you schedule the meeting, clarify your reason. Let the advisor know your specific purpose for the meeting. This

will allow her to have answers before you get there and allow for more discussion time. Remember, she probably has a meeting right after yours.

3. Communicate problems early. Advisors are great at helping solve problems. However, they are limited in their ability to identify them (for the reasons we previously discussed).

I have tremendous respect for academic advisors. Almost every academic advisor I've ever met has been a dedicated educator. The academic advisor plays a crucial role in helping you navigate your education. If you can manage the day-to-day aspects of your academics, such as time management, course research, and study skills, your advisor will be best utilized for the big-picture strategy items.

"Help Me Help You"

In the movie *Jerry Maguire*, Jerry, played by Tom Cruise, is a frustrated sports agent who begs his prize athlete to "*Help me help you!*" This is how I often felt as an advisor. What follows is a common scenario I encountered during my advisor days.

A student makes an appointment and comes to my office to discuss "not doing well in school." We have thirty minutes. We spend twenty-five minutes discussing what "not doing well" means and five minutes brainstorming resolutions. That's a terribly inefficient meeting for both the student and advisor. However, once I trained my students to be proactive, our meetings went more like this: I receive an e-mail scheduling an appointment to discuss a "difficulty in calculus." I confirm the meeting and allot thirty minutes for that student. Prior to the meeting, I have a list of tutors and campus resources ready to help the student (as there's no way I can help them with calculus). Because the student communicated with me prior to the meeting and with a specific topic, we saved the entire thirty minutes for discussion and strategizing.

The take-away message? Communicate early and specifically with your advisor to allow enough time to discuss big-picture topics. You'll be helping the advisor help you!

Summary

My passion for education is matched by my desire to achieve my goal of creating more self-reliant students. No matter how good an advisor I am, I know that the less my students need me, the better off they are. I also understand that no matter how much time your advisor is willing to spend with you, you will still manage the vast majority of your college time on your own. A self-reliant student accepts that he or she is now in the driver's seat. In high school, the ownership of your success is shared between you, your parents, and your teachers. In the military, you had officers and senior enlisted leaders guiding your daily routine. Your success was most often team based. In college, you own your success. Many of your professors will be exceptional educators, but their commitment will be to the class as a unit and not to the individual student. I realized early on in my advising career that the greatest thing any teacher can do to help students is to teach them how to help themselves. No two students are alike, and no two student schedules are alike. You are the one and only person on campus dedicated to your curriculum and your curriculum only. There is no one else with that as a sole responsibility. Advisors, professors, and staff are spread thin over many students. Strategic planning and self-reliance are your keys to success. Make a plan. Follow it. Be prepared to adjust it when circumstances change- because they will.

Did your operations in the military ever go exactly as planned? Probably not. But military precision is still achieved because while the plan gave you the right general direction, you subsequently adjusted your tactics based on real-time information. Your academics will follow a similar cycle. Strategy is your big picture, and tactics are your day-to-day skills.

Chapter 3

Managing Your Grade Point Average: Think Like a Triathlete

Without self-discipline, success is impossible, period.
—Lou Holtz

With so much of college academics being self-managed, it's crucial that students plan study time with their entire portfolio of classes in mind. Specifically, students must retrain themselves to think about how planning affects their semester GPA first and foremost. Individual class grades are a secondary concern. Veterans must realize that they are no longer part of a platoon, company, squadron, or unit. Your pursuit is no longer team-oriented (although you will likely have some team assignments); your class schedule and GPA are yours and yours alone. The feeling of isolation in academics is one of the most difficult obstacles I see veterans face. We come from place where the team is valued above the individual, and most veterans miss that team-centric feeling. However, the quicker you understand your new environment, the less likely this feeling of isolation will drag you down College can be a selfish environment, but that isolated feeling goes away as you engage your mentor network and, quite frankly, as you succeed.

Most students focus on individual classes, and this often leads them to lean toward their strengths when in fact they should be leaning toward their weaknesses. You may be thinking, *But individual class grades are incorporated into GPA, right?* True, but this is only part of the story, and this is where college grading differs from high school grading.

Most colleges grade on a 4.0 scale. Your semester GPA is a *weighted average*. For those who need a little algebra refresher, a weighted average means that classes don't contribute equally to your GPA. Each class is "weighted" by the number of credit hours. Table 3.1 shows how letter grades are correlated to GPA.

Table 3.1. Correlation of letter grades to GPA (based on a 4.0 scale)

Grade Range	Letter Grade	GPA
93–100	A	4.0
90–92	A-	3.67
87–89	B+	3.33
83–86	B	3.00
80–82	B-	2.67
77–79	C+	2.33
73–76	C	2.00
70–72	C-	1.67
67–69	D+	1.33
63–66	D	1.00
60–62	D-	0.67
<60	F	0.00

Two factors should help you shift your mind-set from thinking in terms of class grades to focusing on semester GPA:

1. *Credit hours*—All classes don't have the same credit hours. Some do but not all. Therefore, classes with more credits are going to have a much greater impact than those with less. For example, a class with a lab is worth more credit than a class that's just classroom time.

2. *GPA scale*—Percentage grades or letter grades matter much less in college than in high school. In college, a 100 percent in a class or a 94 percent are no different—each results in a student getting a 4.0 GPA. Likewise, an 83 percent or an 86 percent each gets a student a GPA of 3.0. In high school, it's highly likely that your class rank was your competitive focus. Therefore, a few percentage points in a class could mean a great deal in terms of your rank. I don't know of any colleges that have class rank. In college, your focus is GPA. If two students apply to medical school and both have a 4.0, no one will know who had the 96 percent and who had the 100 percent. Therefore, in managing your GPA, you want to think of your entire schedule of classes as a whole instead of looking at your classes individually.

Tracking Your GPA Like a Triathlete

I love sports, and I love metaphors. As a teacher, it always seemed easier for me to explain a subject by talking about a completely separate one. Sports provide an applicable metaphor for teamwork, determination, skill, and work ethic. I also like that sports have measurable results. Everything is quantified in sports, just like in academics.

Students seem to connect with the metaphors even if they're not athletes (you don't need to be). When I teach students about GPA management, my metaphor of choice is the triathlete.

A triathlon consists of a sequential swim, bike, and run event. The fastest racer across the finish line wins. Simple enough, right? Actually, there's a lot more strategy than that. Triathletes are endurance athletes, much like swimmers, marathoners, and cyclists. The thing that makes triathletes unique is that they're not necessarily that great at any one event compared to athletes who specialize in single events. If the gold medalist triathlete were to compete against Lance Armstrong in cycling, he'd most certainly lose. If he were to compete against Michael Phelps in a swim, he'd lose again. If a triathlete is focusing on setting a world record in the swim, I'd say she's doing "too well" in swimming and needs to shift her focus to the other two events. There's no reason to "win" the swim and then struggle in the bike and run segments and ultimately lose the race. Triathletes are trying to be very good at three events, not record-setting at a single event.

Even though triathletes are generalists, most still have an event they are strongest in and one they are weakest in. If I had to choose one event to be the best in, I'd choose cycling because it counts the most. Cycling is about 50 percent of the race, the run is about 40 percent, and the swim is about 10 percent.

Just like the fact that a triathlete has a stronger event, he or she will also have a weaker event, which will require more training. The reason should be obvious—that event needs more work. A triathlete will track training progress in each event prior to the race to measure progress against goals (this is a subject we'll return to in chapter 4). Tracking is essential in the training of a triathlete.

In the 2009 Ironman Triathlon Championship (Kona, Hawaii), Craig Alexander won the entire race. He wasn't a top-three finisher in either the swim or the bike portion. He didn't need to be because the individuals who dominated the swim and bike segments didn't do as well in their other two events and Craig passed them all at some point. He never lost focus after "losing" the swim and bike portions; he just kept pace and ran his race. Craig wasn't trying to be the world's best swimmer, cyclist, or runner. He was trying to be the world's best triathlete, and he accomplished just that.

How does this relate to academics? I want you to think like a triathlete. I especially want you to think like Craig Alexander. More specifically:

- **Be a generalist**. It's better to be very good in all your classes than to be great in a few classes and weak in others. The triathlete is focused on one data point: finishing time. *You need to focus on one data point: GPA.* No graduate school or future employer will ask you if you scored the highest grades in any single class. They will ask what your GPA is. No one cares who won the swim if that athlete isn't on the podium at the end of the day.

- **Don't compete in individual classes.** It's easy to get caught up in class competition. Craig never got caught up trying to "win" the bike or swim portion of the triathlon. If he had, he wouldn't have had enough energy left in the run to win the race. Remember, there's no point getting the highest grade in one class if your other classes are suffering.
- **Focus on higher credit-hour classes.** Just as the cycling segment counts for "more" in a triathlon, higher credit-hour classes count for more in your GPA. If your classes aren't equal in terms of credit hours, focus on the class with the higher number of credit hours. This will have a magnified effect on your GPA (both positively and negatively).
- **Train more in more difficult classes.** Like a triathlete who isn't equally proficient in all three events, you probably won't be equally proficient in all of your classes. A triathlete who's a weaker runner will run more in training than he or she will bike or swim. Similarly, you'll need to work more in a subject you're weaker in. The important point here is to know your strengths and weaknesses. I'll discuss how to determine that in chapter 4.

Thinking like a triathlete is way of reminding you what the goal is: GPA, GPA, and GPA. You don't have to be the best student in any one class, nor should you be. Your finish line is the aggregate of all of your classes. Think like Craig Alexander: set your pace, and then win the race. No one remembers who won the swim leg.

Why Is GPA More Important than Percentage Grades?

Thinking like a triathlete will affect your academic success and competiveness. This section highlights why your GPA is so important.

One semester, one of my students came to me with his grades, which are shown in table 3.2. Alex earned a highly respectable 3.6 GPA and was quite pleased with himself.

Table 3.2. Alex's Grades

Class	Percent-age Grade	Letter Grade	Credit Hours	GPA	Quality Points (Credit Hours x GPA)
Writing	99	A	3	4.00	12.00
Calculus	89	B+	4	3.33	13.32
Biology (w/ Lab)	89	B+	5	3.33	16.65
US History	99	A	3	4.00	12.00
Semester Total:			15	3.60*	53.97

Semester GPA = Total Quality Points (53.97) divided by Total Credit Hours (15): 53.96/15 = 3.60

The first thing I said to Alex was, "You could have done much better."

Alex's face dropped, and he said, "But I got a 3.6!"

I responded, "Yes, I can see that." I went on to explain that with no additional time spent, he should have had a 3.80 GPA. Here's my reasoning: Alex's two lowest grades (albeit very good grades) were in high-credit-hour classes (calculus and biology were 4 and 5, respectively). Alex did too well in history and writing. That's right—too well.

Alex responded somewhat defeated, "I didn't think there was such a thing as 'too well,' " he said. "I got the highest grade in the history class, and the professor loves me." He was so proud of getting the highest grade, and my telling him he could have done better overall wasn't easy.

Alex got a 99 percent in writing and history. If he had studied the same amount of total time, yet shifted a portion of hours from writing/history to calculus/biology, I suspect his transcript would have looked like Ella's, another student who took similar classes (table 3.3). I showed him Ella's grades (after covering up her name).

Table 3.3. Ella's Grades

Class	Number Grade	Letter Grade	Credit Hours	GPA	Quality Points (Credit Hours x GPA)
Writing	95	A	3	4.00	12.00
Calculus	90	A-	4	3.67	14.68
Biology (w/ Lab)	90	A-	5	3.67	18.38
US History	95	A	3	4.00	12.00
Semester Total:			15	3.80*	57.06

Semester GPA of 3.80 = 57.06/15, or Total Quality Points/Credit Hours

What a difference! If you're competing for a spot in a competitive graduate school, a 3.8 GPA is significantly better than a 3.6. Alex felt even worse when I explained that if one looked merely at percentage scores, he actually beat Ella. Alex's semester percentage grade (weighted average) was 93 percent, and Ella's was 92 percent. Yet her GPA was much higher! If you looked at classes individually as a win or a loss, Alex got the higher grade in two classes and Ella got the higher grade in two classes (table 3.4).

Alex far surpassed Ella in writing and history, while Ella beat Alex in calculus and biology by one point each. Yet, in the end, Ella won the race by quite a bit. Now you see how *GPA instead of percentage grades truly changes the game.*

You can receive higher letter grades overall than another student and still receive a lower GPA.

Table 3.4. A Comparison of Alex's and Ella's Grades

Class	Alex's % Grade	Ella's % Grade	Winner
Writing	99	95	Alex by 4.0 points!
Calculus	89	90	Ella by 1.0 point!
Biology	89	90	Ella by 1.0 point!
US History	99	95	Alex by 4.0 points!
Semester Grade	93%*	92%**	Alex by 1.0 Point!
GPA	3.60	3.80	*Ella by 0.2!*

* Alex's 93% = [(99x3) + (89x4) + (89x5) + (99x3)]/15 credits
**Ella's 92% = [(95x3) + (90x4) + (90x5) + (95x3)]/15 credits

Alex then asked a really good question, "What if all our classes were equal in credit hours? Should I think the same way?" The answer is yes. If all of the classes were the same credit hours, Ella still would have come out on top; the effect would just not have been as magnified. If all the classes were three credit hours, Ella would have received a 3.84 and Alex would have received a 3.67 (see table 3.5). This is still a very big difference for no additional work. With even credit hours, the effect of GPA management is less magnified but still apparent. Ella still wins.

I explained to Alex that if he approached his academics like Ella and stopped worrying about getting the highest grade possible in any class, he'd do much better. The best part is he wouldn't have to spend any more time studying. He'd simply need to adjust his strategy with the semester GPA in mind and *not* percentage grades.

Table 3.5. Alex and Ella's GPA Comparison If All Classes Are Equal Credit Hours

Class	Credits	Alex's Letter Grades	Alex's Quality Points	Ella's Letter Grades	Ella's Quality Points
Writing	3	A	12.00	A	12.00
Calculus	3	B+	9.99	A-	11.01
Biology	3	B+	9.99	A-	11.01
US History	3	A	12.00	A	12.00
Total	12		43.98		46.02
GPA		3.67		3.84	

Like the triathlete, you don't need to win a single event, nor should you try. You're out to win the whole race. Remember, a GPA is not actually a perfect score of 100 percent; it's only 93 percent. The goal of a strategic student is not to be perfect but rather just be very good at multiple courses simultaneously.

Summary

Military veterans almost universally appreciate and respect the concept of intelligence and strategy; yet they often fail to translate this mind-set to their college academic environment. Guess what. It works as well on campus as it does on the battlefield. This chapter is about the intelligence needed to develop a strategy. Our next chapters are about strategy, tactics, and implementation. The goal of this chapter was also to get you to think like a triathlete. To a student, this means two goals. The first goal was to help you understand the transition from letter (percentage) grades to GPA. The second goal was to help you view your academics as a portfolio of all of your classes and not as individual pursuits. The world will judge your academic performance by one data point, GPA. Understanding GPA management will help you implement a strong academic strategy designed to help you win the whole race, not just one event.

PART TWO

Academic Skills for Success

Chapter 4

Time Management: Creating an Effective Study Hours Plan

Time equals life; therefore, waste your time and
waste your life, or master your time and master your life.
—Alan Lakein

The most powerful thing you can do to become an academic ace is master time management. Time management is very different for a college student than for it is for the military professional who's simply trying to get more out of the day. In college, you have the time, but the challenge lies in estimating the necessary study time and efficiently executing a study plan. Unfortunately, standard time-management practices don't address the college student's needs.

The strategic student time-management system is unique. In this chapter, we'll look at some effective ways of estimating your study time, scheduling it, and tracking your progress. All of my successful students used some variation of this system as a progress measuring stick. This chapter offers a lot of advice. At the very least, skim the contents. When you're ready to build your study plan, come back and reread the chapter and complete the time-management worksheet. After completing your worksheet, you will have your starting point for building a highly effective study plan.

Inefficient Time-Management Practices

Before we look at the best practices for time management, let's look at three of the most common, though highly *ineffective*, practices that students use for studying: event-driven studying, sporadic studying, and studying until you "feel good." My purpose in pointing out these inefficiencies is to help you steer clear of them at all costs! It can be tempting to look around at your classmates and simply follow the crowd. Your reward is during midterms and at the end of the semester when your traditional student classmates are using words like *cramming* and *all-nighter*. These are the words of unprepared students who are dead in the water and don't even know it yet. During finals and midterms, these students will be wondering why you seemingly don't study that much and don't appear too stressed. In fact, you should never have to resort to marathon study sessions, and I'll show you why.

Event-Driven Studying

Most freshmen will study based on events immediately in front of them. For example, let's say a student has a chemistry test this Thursday and nothing due in any other classes. This week, that student will likely study exclusively for chemistry. Although many freshmen do well at first using this approach and actually get a few good grades, the approach starts a negative ripple effect that won't be realized until further down the road.

If you devote all your time to one class, you ignore your other classes for a period of time. So the next week you ignore chemistry and study for your economics test, and then the next week, you switch over to another class, and so on. Now when your second chemistry test rolls around, a few weeks will have passed where you haven't looked at chemistry. This is a tremendous problem because it's going to take significant time to review and get your rhythm back. You may even have to refresh your knowledge of material that's a few weeks old yet necessary to know for today's material. Moreover, if you've sat in class for a few weeks without having read the assigned material, you've spent even more time ineffectively.

What happens if you have multiple graded events in the same week or, heaven forbid, on the same day? When you have a week with multiple graded evaluations like a paper due, a test, and a project, you are in serious trouble. There's no way to catch up. An events-driven approach to studying is extremely imbalanced and does not allow for multiple-test weeks—which *will* happen. A balanced approach to studying means that you set aside week-ly study time in each one of your classes so that you'll remain prepared (more on creating a balanced approach later in this chapter).

Sporadic Studying

Sporadic studying is also a form of imbalance. This imbal-ance means that students are not distributing the quantity of their studying over the course of the whole semester. It's feast or fam-ine. Tough weeks are followed by easy weeks. I teach students to spread the work over all fifteen weeks of the semester—to have fifteen "medium" weeks.

Students tend to think that a semester is very long, and there-fore, they're entitled to warm-up time at the beginning of the se-mester and downtime after a major test or project. In other words, they wind up and they wind down similar to the jagged line in figure 4.1. This sporadic method would be like a marathon runner sprinting for a mile and then walking for mile and repeating until he or she finishes the race. The strategy does not work because it's an inefficient use of energy and time. Runners, like students, are aiming for efficiency, which is why you don't see a marathon run-ner ever running a sprint-walk-style race. Instead, you see evenly paced miles with a slight increase in pace toward the end of the race.

Study Hours per Week during a Semester

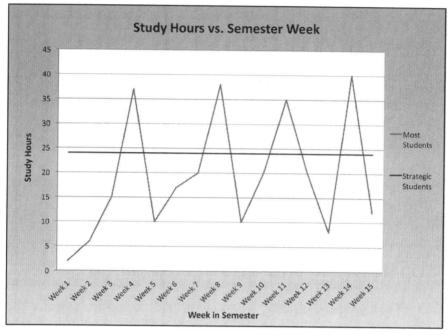

Figure 4.1. The jagged line represents average students while the straight line represents strategic students. The strategic student balances study hours over the whole semester.

Trust me, at some point in your college career, you'll hear a student say something along the lines of, "I studied fifteen hours yesterday for this test." There is no reason ever to study that much in one day…especially the same subject matter. That student is doing it wrong.

Students as Tight-Rope Walkers

Imagine you are standing on a tight rope. If you remain steady, you can probably stay balanced for a long period of time. Now picture yourself starting to swing a little. You shift your weight to compensate for the swing. With each subsequent weight shift, the swing to the opposite side magnifies. Now you are standing on a rope swinging back and forth and your chances of falling are steadily increasing.

It's not the first swing that knocks you off the rope. The first swing causes a ripple effect, and it is a large swing later on that causes the fall. The student who studies sporadically and/or based only on the events of the week is starting a ripple effect. At first, it's no big deal, but as the semester continues and he keeps chasing classes, the effect worsens.

The individual who keeps her weight equally distributed on both sides of the rope stays balanced longer. The balanced student distributes her time strategically among all classes and studies toward that goal every week. The balanced student is much more difficult to knock off the rope and therefore is more successful.

Studying until You "Feel Good"

When I became an experienced pilot in my navy squadron, I used to roll my eyes when I heard junior pilots make statements along the lines of, "I feel good about this plan." Their intentions were good, but their feelings weren't trustworthy yet. The accuracy of instinctive decisions is directly related to the decision-maker's experience level. In other words, a gunnery sergeant's instincts are significantly more reliable than a lance corporal's.

As a college freshman, your experience level is at its lowest possible level. (Remember, high school or military success doesn't guarantee college success.) Therefore, going by what feels right can and will mislead you because you have no collegiate frame of reference to base your feelings and instincts on. Don't feel bad; we've all been there. When you're a college senior or even a junior, your ability to go by feel will be greatly enhanced because you'll be more experienced. For now, think of your feelings as little liars.

Even great students run into problems with going by feel. Top-caliber students may never truly feel good about their prepared-ness and therefore will keep studying right up until test time. They get a great grade on their test, but they've ignored other classes, exercise, social life, and/or work, and have returned to being im-balanced. The ripple effect follows.

What Is Student Time Management?

Student time management is a system that will help you deal with academic ambiguity and maintain balance between all of your classes. Freshman students make a common mistake and think that they can go by "feel" because perhaps they did so well in high school and in the military. This approach doesn't work for most and sets many up for failure.

In the military, you do most of your learning in training; it's very hands-on (that's why it's so fun!). In college, you do most of your learning in your "free time." In high school, you have specific homework assignments, and by doing these assignments, you solidify classroom learning. Test preparation is built into the system. If you aren't doing your homework, then you aren't preparing for tests, and the teacher is onto you. High school is designed to identify at-risk students before problems become too severe. This works well, and we have many amazing high-school teachers to thank for executing this system every day.

College students accept a major level of academic autonomy—often without realizing it. This autonomy is necessary for academic growth, but it's also largely due to the fact there are simply more students (thousands in some cases). Professors don't have time to be constantly grading assignments—one class can have hundreds of students. In reality, college students don't even have that many assignments to turn in for grading. This is true even at smaller schools.

Many first-year students think that time management is added work. Nothing could be further from the truth. *The goal of a solid time-management strategy is to streamline your work* so you spend less time studying. Spending a minute or two a day on time management will actually save you many hours during the week.

The Strategic Student Time-Management System

Many time-management strategies for students involve checklists of tasks and assignments. Making lists of assignments and checking things off is helpful if you have defined homework, but it won't give you the whole picture and can even mislead you.

In college, there are many periods of time (weeks even) where you may not have specific assignments, projects, or tests. This often gives students a false sense of comfort and free time. The reason this comfort is false is because those classes without assignments still require a steady supply of attention. College is about learning and is not always defined by specific homework assignments. Learning can take the shape of studying, reading, group meetings, practice problems, organizing, and other activities.

Estimate—Execute—Track—Repeat

The strategic student time-management system includes four simple steps:

1. **Estimate—Determine an estimate for weekly study time needed per class.** You won't find this key step in other time-management programs. Before the semester starts, you'll estimate how much study time per week you'll need for each of your classes. This will give you a goal to track your progress against. I will teach you how to estimate your study hours later in this chapter.
2. **Execute—Carry out and focus on "quality" study hours.** You'll learn how to balance the quality of study time with the quantity of study time in this chapter and in chapter 5.
3. **Track—Incorporate a method for tracking study hours by class**. Have you ever been lost on a field navigation exercise? The first step in reaching your destination is to first figure out where you are currently located. Tracking allows you to compare where you are versus where you want to be. Tracking will also prevent you from getting lost in the first place. A tracking method needs to be simple and not take up much time. The last thing a student needs is another project.

4. **Repeat—Adjust your study plan as the semester moves forward.** Your presemester estimate will get you in the ballpark. Now you're going to fine-tune your study plan in order to even further focus your time allocation. By the end of the semester, you'll have a strong sense of how much time is needed per class every week.

Time Management: Antidote to Stress

Stress is your mortal enemy in college. You'll hear traditional students talk about how stressed they are all the time. Student veterans tend to laugh at this. These "stressed" students are the same students who will wonder why you're well rested on test day when they spent the night cramming information for ten hours (about one hour of which was effective). Stress inhibits your learning and can cause even highly intelligent students to score low on tests. It's also preventable. Time management is your most powerful weapon against stress.

Time management even makes your free time better. Let's say you're tracking your study hours and you're right on schedule in terms of your study plan. Your downtime is exactly what it's supposed to be: relaxing, fun, and reenergizing. But what if you're not tracking your study hours and you've taken a few days off from studying? Now you hear that little nasty voice in the back of your head telling you that the mountain of work is growing and growing. The latter situation is stressful, and you're not really enjoying yourself. You're actually building more stress during your downtime—the complete opposite of what downtime should be. Time management doesn't just help you get higher grades; it makes your free time even better!

Balancing Quantity and Quality of Studying Time

Outstanding grades in college are the result of efficient learning by putting in the right amount of time *and no more.* Over-studying is to be avoided as well because if you over-study, you'll burn out and ignore other classes and activities.

A few students have said to me, "It's not about the quantity of study hours; it's about the quality." Some best-selling study-skills books reinforce the same notion. The fact is, it's about both. I concede that quality is more important, but quantity is not to be neglected.

To convince students of this, I offer them a challenge. Let's say there are two students, Tim and Amy. These students have identical academic aptitude, and they're in the same Biology 101 class together. The quality of their study hours is rated using standard letter grades (A, B, C...). Amy studies for ten grade-A-quality hours for the midterm, and Tim studies for one grade-A-quality hour. I then ask the class, "Who do you think will get the higher grade, Tim or Amy?" I always get 100 percent votes for Amy. We all agree that the time committed is absolutely correlated to grades.

To say it's only about the quality of studying is ridiculous. Don't let anyone tell you not to study hard; you have to put in your time. You have to be disciplined and study the minimum amount to reach your goal. If your goal is an A, the minimum amount of study time will still be a substantial number of hours (same for a B). Imagine if an Olympic swimmer only trained one day a month and stated, "But it was a really high-quality training session." I would bet on her to lose every race.

Think of academic success as a three-legged stool: one leg is quantity of study time, one leg is quality of study time, and the third leg is class time. Neglect any one of the three legs, and things get very wobbly. Again, I believe that the quality of study hours is the most important leg, but it doesn't independently make for academic success.

Time management is all about the right quantity of quality study hours and no more.

Time Management Levels the Playing Field

High school segregates classes into levels because they want the whole class to move through the material at a similar pace. Classes meet almost every day, and tests, homework, and quizzes are very frequent. In high school, the "quicker" student has the advantage in terms of scoring high grades. However, in college, your class will meet only two to three times a week and graded assignments are not nearly as frequent.

How does this relate to time management? It doesn't matter how quickly you learn the material in college as long as you learn it before the graded event (test, quiz, etc.). Who cares if a "more intelligent" student "got it quicker" than you? That quicker student's only advantage is he or she may have to study less, but you can both get an A. In college, you can be less intimidated by that super-smart kid from your high-school class.

Let's look at a quick example. You are in Calculus, and you have class on Tuesday and Thursday. It's Thursday. Marty McSmarty Pants, who sits next to you in class, really "gets it" right away, and you do not. You ask yourself, "Shouldn't I get it too?" Being the strategic student that you are, you go study at a few intervals over the next four days, and by Tuesday, you too "get it." Your slower pace didn't hurt you because you have the time in college and if you use it strategically, you will get to the exact same place as Marty. This is the main reason why I think an A is well within the reach of any student on campus if he or she is an effective manager of time.

Study Hours: Achieving the Right Balance

Study hours are a broad term I use to mean any amount of time you devote to a particular class. That time could be reading, practicing problems, e-mailing classmates, or doing research—basically any time you spend doing "something" productive for that class, not just studying in the traditional sense.

When I was an undergraduate student, almost every professor communicated a recommendation for a number of weekly study hours. It was usually embedded in the syllabus, something worded along the lines of "two to three hours per every hour in class." When

I became a graduate student, the same guideline appeared in many of my classes. This is when I began to scratch my head. How could every class have the same recommendation? And how could a professor know how much I needed to study without knowing me, my aptitude, or my goals? I've asked my undergraduate students if I could see their syllabi, and as you can imagine, the same line was often there. *Colleges generally recommend two to three hours of studying per every hour in class.* Here are my issues with this rule of thumb.

Why You Should *Not* "Study Two to Three Hours for Each Hour in Class"

The equation is unrealistic. If you take only one or two classes, then studying two to three hours per class hour is doable. However, full-time students usually take four or five classes. The following example shows why the generally recommended studying equation is unrealistic.

Mandy is taking five classes, a normal course load that wouldn't raise any red flags for her advisor. Each class meets three hours per week. If Mandy follows the college rule of thumb, which means her university is asking her to *study forty-five hours a week (5 classes x 3 hours class time x 3 hours study time).* Is this realistic? Of course not! Throw in a work-study job, sports practice, club involvement, exercise, and maybe even sleep, and there simply isn't enough time in the week. *A strategic student needs to think in terms of his or her whole schedule when forming a study plan.* This is a theme I will continue to revisit.

Your goals aren't considered. When a professor recommends two to three hours of study time per in-class hour, this number is not correlated to any specific results (grades). Is this advice for students seeking an A? Or are the two to three hours the average amount of study time, which implies that your goal is the class average? If your goal is to get an A, I'd interpret the rule of thumb to mean you need to study more than the average. However, if you're taking an elective class pass/fail, you wouldn't want to study the same amount as you would for the classes in which you're seeking an A; you'd want to study *less* in order to redirect your time toward studying for the graded classes.

The same studying rule won't work for all classes. No two students possess the same aptitude, strengths, and weaknesses; every student's learning needs and styles vary. So to apply the same studying rule to all students in all classes is a one-size-fits-all approach that's doomed to fail. We are all very different. I'll use myself as example. I'm a slow reader. I've tried various techniques to increase my speed, but this fact remains true. When I was an undergraduate, I probably required more time than the average student to read assignments. But because I'm quick with math, I may have required less time than the average student in math-based classes. The point is that self-assessment is an essential part of determining how much study time you'll really need.

If you had infinite time in the week, I wouldn't even discuss this subject. I would recommend studying three hours for every hour in class. But the fact is you are dealing with a limited budget of time, which does not allow for a blanket approach to study planning.

Personalizing Your Study Hours

The strategic student's goal before registering for classes is to make an assessment of how much studying will be required to reach his or her goals in each class. It's a difficult task, but it's a crucial one. It will alert you to the difficulties that lie ahead. If you know what's coming, it's much easier to prepare. It will also alert you to the fact that you might be taking too light of a schedule. (Graduate schools don't like students taking the easy road.) The strategic student is always seeking balance. For example, if you identify that your fall semester is lighter on study time than your spring semester, you may decide to schedule volunteer work or extra research time in the fall and focus more on studying in the spring. Perhaps you'll want to swap a fall class with a spring class. The key is to know (or have an idea) of what's inbound. You don't want to find out midsemester that you're overloaded. An assessment worksheet, which will help you determine your personalized study hours, is provided later in this chapter.

Thinking Ahead Saves Money

Students who drop classes past the deadline do *not* get a refund. Thousands of GI Bill dollars are lost if you start and drop a class midsemester. Every semester, I see at least one student drop a class because the student feels "overloaded." (I'm guilty of having done the same thing in college.) It's not that these students can't handle their class; it's that they can't handle it with everything else going on in their lives. Figure this out beforehand, and big money will be saved.

Determining Your Study-Hour Plan

Calculating a study-hour estimate is a highly individualized process and also differs by school. As an advisor, I'd sit down with students prior to the semester and conduct this exercise in person. Don't expect your advisor to do this; it takes a while, and they have too many students. I was able to do this because I had only about forty ROTC students a semester. While I can't deliver a single formula applicable to every student, I can discuss the theory behind the process and give you a general blueprint to follow.

This approach is both quantitative and qualitative. Because the process is so individualized, it can also be time-consuming. Software I'm developing to help students customize their own study plan will take a few seconds and will be more accurate. Until that's available, you can follow the steps outlined in the next section and do a similar self-assessment. I recommend skimming the section first, thinking about it, and completing the questions after you've read the rest of the book, especially chapter 5, "Study Skills." The six steps of the assessment process are:

1. Assess your aptitude (skills dominance) and interests.
2. Determine the skills dominance of your classes.
3. Review students' average study hours per class.
4. Adjust the study-hour rule of thumb.
5. Determine extracurricular hours.
6. Total your study and extracurricular hours.

Six-Step Self-Assessment Process (Worksheet to Follow)

1. **Assess your aptitude (skills dominance) and interests**.

   The goal of this step is to determine if you're math/science oriented, reading/writing oriented, or have a "balanced" orientation (equally incorporating both math and verbal skills). It's important to note that *none of these categories is better or worse than the others*—but understanding what subjects you're dominant in is key to helping you personalize your study plan.

   Ask yourself the following questions:

   A. Would you rather take a test or write a paper?
   B. Would you rather read a book or do math problems for homework?
   C. What were your SAT scores? ACT scores?

   Your answers to questions A and B reveal what types of classes you like. If you don't like the subject material, you probably won't enjoy learning it and most likely will not do well. If you answered that you'd rather write a paper and you prefer reading, you're probably a *verbally oriented student* and would be more comfortable in qualitative classes, such as history, writing, political science, or literature (to name a few). If you prefer taking tests and doing math problems, you're probably a *mathematically oriented student* and would be most comfortable in math, engineering, and science classes. If one of your answers to questions A and B indicate math dominance and the other indicates verbal dominance, you may be a balanced student—a business strategy class or microeconomics might appeal to you—or you can use your answer to question C, your standardized test scores, to determine your dominance. Remember, no answer is the "right" answer. This takes some interpretation.

   I think standardized tests are a lousy measure of student intelligence. However, I do believe they're an excellent measurement of a student's skills dominance. Does your math percentile differ from either of your verbal scores (reading or writing) by 10 percentile points or more? If so, the higher of the scores indicates dominance. For example, Eric scored in the eightieth percentile in reading, the ninetieth percentile in writing, and the sixty-seventh percentile in math. Eric is a verbally dominant student because at least one of his verbal scores is greater than 10 percentile points higher than his math score (80 − 67 = 13). While this equation is by no means definitive, your answers to questions A through C should enable you to categorize yourself as one of three types of students:

1) mathematically dominant
2) verbally dominant
3) balanced

2. **Determine the skills dominance of your classes.**

Study hours need to be determined per class per person. Therefore, before registration, read the class description and determine if the class is mathematically dominant, verbally dominant, or balanced in both skills.

3. **Review students' average study hours per class**.

Many schools have a course critique system. As part of this system, students are often asked how much time they spent studying outside of class time. The results are averaged, but by looking up each class you'll be taking, you'll get a rough idea of the time commitment necessary to meet your course goals. I hope your school has this database available. If not, try asking for it. Warning: faculty course critiques are valuable but should be taken with a degree of caution. Students often have a bias toward/against instructors. For example, "Easy A" professors often get great reviews. On the contrary, very challenging yet great professors often receive poor ratings. For our purposes, checking to assess the study-time commitment per class is a worthwhile exercise, and I have found this data point alone to be very valuable.

4. **Adjust the study-hours rule of thumb.**

At this point, you've collected valuable information on yourself, your class, and previous students. Now you'll want to adjust the rule of thumb in order to create a more reasonable study plan. Keep in mind that changes from moving the rule of thumb right or left even a little bit really accumulate over the course of a week.

- Assume a starting point of two hours of studying per hour in class.
- Increase study hours if you're weak in the subject matter or if previous students reported greater than two hours of study time per class hour.
- Add two hours a week for any laboratory class.
- Decrease study hours if the class subject matter is your strength *or* if previous students reported studying less than two hours per class hour *or* if you're taking the class pass/fail.

Figure 4.2 is a visualization of your movement. Adjust your study hours up or down as you see fit. Recommendations:

- Don't increase beyond three hours of studying per every hour in class. For example, if your statistics class meets for three hours a week, studying more than nine hours *(3 class hours x 3 study hours)* could adversely affect your other classes.
- Don't decrease beyond one hour of studying per every hour in class.
- Keep adjusting as the semester moves forward. Reassess at midsemester.

Determining Study Hours

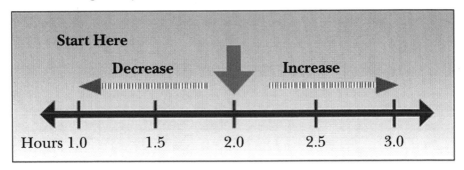

Figure 4.2. Determining study hours is a matter of personalizing the rule of thumb.

5. **Determine extracurricular hours.**

Tally the amount of hours spent per week doing the following activities:

- working at a job
- involvement in clubs or sports
- exercise
- other commitments outside of class

6. **Total your study and extracurricular hours.**

The following worksheet will help you accumulate this data. Simply add up your study and extracurricular hours and consult the results beneath the table to determine the feasibility of your study plan's success. (External to your scheduled class, study, and exercise time, it doesn't really matter how you spend your time, whether it's on chores, sleeping, shopping, personal hygiene, video games…whatever.)

Don't be overwhelmed by what is actually simple logic. The whole process in a nutshell is: *assess your aptitude and interests, assess the class, assess your school, adjust the study-hours rule of thumb, and execute.*

Table 4.1. Time-Management Worksheet

Question	Answer
1. Are you a mathematically dominant, verbally dominant, or balanced student?	
2. Is your class mathematically dominant, verbally dominant, or balanced?	
Example: Calculus	Mathematically dominant
Class 1:	
Class 2:	
Class 3:	
Class 4:	
Class 5:	
3. Enter class name, the number of study hours per class hour you determined, and your weekly in-class hours in the following form (Class Title / Study hours / In-class hours). Multiply study hours and in-class-hours to determine your total weekly study-hour goal.	
Example: Econ 101/ 2 hours study / 3 hours class time	6 hours of weekly study (2 x 3)
Class 1:	
Class 2:	
Class 3:	
Class 4:	
Class 5:	
3. Total	
4. How many hours a week are you in class?	
5. How many hours a week do you work a job?	
6. How many hours a week do you exercise?	
7. How many hours a week in organized extracurricular activities, such as clubs, sports, ROTC, etc.?	
8. Any other time commitments outside of class?	
Total Hours (add up numbers 3–8)	

Worksheet results: What do your total hours mean?

< 45 hours: High probability of success

45–55 hours: Semester is feasible, but proceed with caution

> 55 hours: Low probability of success

> The most effective time-management strategy in college is to schedule your study time first and fill in your study tasks/assignments second.

Calendaring

Keeping a calendar is simple, but surprisingly, I found most students don't keep one, or if they do, they don't use it effectively. A calendar's power is in its ability to keep you out of trouble. My advice: go high-tech!

I'm quite surprised at the number of paper or binder-type calendars I see students still using and the number of study books that still recommend them. It's no secret that I dislike these types of calendars. They're time-consuming. They're messy (you can't easily move events around). And what if you lose it? Granted, you're better off using a paper or binder-type calendar than no calendar, but an electronic calendar can save you headaches via its editing and viewing options.

Electronic Calendars

Strategic students use software and/or web-based calendars for three main reasons. First, you can centralize your events with your laptop, mobile device, or tablet and update your events in one place but be able to reference them anywhere. Microsoft Outlook for PCs and iCal for Macs both work well. Google Calendar is the most popular and easiest to use web-based calendar I have found. There are many offerings out there, and I don't think which one you use matters too much. The key is to be centralized and accessible via all of your devices.

Second, a web-based calendar makes scheduling and tracking study hours a breeze. Study hours don't always go exactly according to schedule; they don't have to. The key is that when you track your hours in a dynamic environment, a digital calendar makes it easy to move events or expand and contract hours.

Third, any software calendar allows you to swap views between day, week, and month. This is essential because it allows you to zoom out for the big picture and zoom in for your day-to-day tactics. Strategic students all share the quality of understanding the big picture while simultaneously executing daily tasks.

Getting the Big Picture

One common error I saw with my students was their constant focus on what was immediately in front of them. They were just trying to get through the day. These students were caught completely unprepared when a busy week came, or worse, two assignments were due on the same day. I remember sitting in my office once with one student, and I said to him something like, "Well, finals are in three weeks."

He shouted, "There are only three weeks left in the semester?" He really had no idea.

Zoom out to a monthly view once a day via your calendar; it will give you the big picture.

Using your calendar

First Week of the Semester

Enter all your scheduled and repeated organized events. Organized events are class periods, club meetings, sports practice, work hours, and so forth. They are not sleep, chores, errands, etc. This is easy to do with software because you only have to enter it once and then include the dates. (Can you imagine doing this on a paper calendar?)

Once you've received your class syllabus, enter all your "due dates." Any time you have a deliverable, put it on the calendar! Tests, papers, projects...all of them go on the calendar. Zoom out on the month views, and you'll instantly see if there's a rough week this semester. Don't worry, though, because you'll be prepared.

Weekly

On Sundays, open up your calendar and scan the month ahead. Then, set it to the week's view. Enter your study hours *by class subject* wherever you choose to. Just make sure the hours add up to your goal number of hours. Remember, you probably won't study exactly how this schedule is written, but this gives you a plan. Knowing when you are on or off the plan is just as valuable as following it explicitly.

Daily

In the evening, open up your calendar to the next day using the day view. Open up your scheduled study hours for each class. Enter the tasks that you'd like to complete in that time period. This calendaring method is helpful because you'll note where you left off on today's events and you'll be reminded where to pick up tomorrow.

Schedule High-Priority Studying Tasks Earlier in the Day

If you find out that a task will take longer than you anticipated, push back other tasks to later (or tomorrow) and use that time to finish your high-priority items.

Enter in your class portion of the schedule what you're doing that day in class. It will remind you to prepare accordingly for the class or at least to bring the lecture notes.

Make a note on your daily tasks where you left off in your studying. Be specific, right down to the page number or concept to review. This will remind you of your starting point the next time you pick up the material. No more spending twenty minutes asking yourself, "Now where was I?"

While you don't have to schedule your personal to-dos, you certainly can. You can also include a to-do list on the bottom of your calendar to include items such as "Call Mom" or "Schedule dentist appointment." You don't need to assign a time for these tasks because you can do them whenever you get a chance. It's helpful to have a list, though.

Most students carry around a mobile device. If you prefer using paper, that's fine. You can print your schedule or just jot it down on a sheet of paper or in a notepad.

Sample Calendars

Calendaring is an essential weapon for your time-management arsenal of skills. Figures 4.3 and 4.4 show two different examples of calendar views. Let's look first at Tim's weekly schedule, which he produced on Sunday.

Tim's Weekly Planner

	6 Sunday	7 Monday	8 Tuesday	9 Wednesday	10 Thursday	11 Friday	12 Saturday
9am		CHEMISTRY 101: Finishing Chapter 3	STUDY	CHEMISTRY 101: Chapter 4 Lecture	STUDY	CHEMISTRY 101: Chapter 4 Lecture	
10:00		STUDY	CALCULUS	STUDY	CALCULUS: Practice Problems Due	STUDY	
11:00	STUDY	ENGLISH LITERATURE		ENGLISH LITERATURE		ENGLISH LITERATURE Paper Proposal Due	
12pm			STUDY				
1:00		STUDY		STUDY	STUDY	STUDY	
2:00			CHEM LAB:				
3:00		US HISTORY	Turn in Lab #3 write-up	US HISTORY	VOLUNTEERS CLUB MEETING	US HISTORY	
4:00		LACROSSE PRACTICE	LACROSSE	LACROSSE PRACTICE	LACROSSE PRACTICE	LACROSSE PRACTICE	
5:00	STUDY		PRACTICE				
6:00							
7:00		STUDY	STUDY	STUDY	STUDY		STUDY
8:00	STUDY						

Figure 4.3. *Tim's weekly schedule.*

Tim's schedule is full. He's taking four classes, he's an athlete, and he's in a club. He totals forty-six hours of hard scheduled events, which puts him in the tough-but-doable range. To increase his odds of success, Tim has made himself a very workable and strategic schedule. Here's how:

Tim determined he needs twenty-four hours a week of studying based on his presemester analysis. He scheduled his weekly study hours without identifying subject matter. That's okay because he can track his class distribution as he goes. Tim is just assigning time now. He never studies more than two hours at a time. He takes advantage of "pockets" of time during the day. Very effective system! He can see his due dates in the weekly view. He leaves only 1.5 hours for evening studying. He can always take more time if he needs it (for example, if he doesn't complete one of his day study sessions). But Tim knows there's nothing worse than being tired at 8:00 p.m. and having four hours of ineffective studying ahead of him, so he aims to complete his day sessions. He has nothing scheduled before 9:00 a.m. because he knows he won't do it. He hasn't scheduled anything past 9:00 p.m. because he knows that's "hangout" time. Tim could hang out from 9:00 until midnight every night stress free if he wants. (His buddies will be doing that regardless, except they'll be talking about all the work they need to do tomorrow!) He doesn't schedule chores and meals because that's tedious and he can see those free blocks of time on his calendar. He can, however, add those tasks on his to-do list. Most often, Tim has sections of time between events. This is a great buffer because it leaves room for unplanned events on his way to studying.

Tim color-codes classes on the calendar and activities for ease of viewing. You can do the same.

Friday evenings and Saturdays are free time. But Tim does take an hour before he heads out on Saturday night to do some light reading. One hour is easy to do.

Sundays Tim is using intervals effectively: a couple of study sessions and lots of the day to play. Nothing is scheduled too early on Sunday. He knows he's going out Saturday night, so why schedule early Sunday morning studying? He'll get up, have coffee, watch a little tube, and then go study for a short session.

Tim's social life is *unaffected by his study schedule.* College social life is at night, and Tim's nights are basically free!

Tim's studying *does not have to go exactly according to this schedule,* but by having a schedule, he knows when he deviates and by how much. Let's say Tim wants to go out Thursday night and he doesn't feel like studying beforehand. No problem. He only loses

1.5 hours of studying. The point is that he's aware of what he's sacrificing, and now he goes out and has a great time because he's not overly stressed. Tim can make that up easily by adding forty-five minutes to two other days in the week, or perhaps he'll spend an additional hour and a half studying on Friday.

> You don't have to follow your study schedule exactly. Knowing you skipped or didn't complete a study session is as valuable as completing the session.

If a monthly view is the big picture on a calendar, then the weekly view is your medium picture. Let's now take a look at a daily/hourly view (figure 4.4). This is your most granular view; it's, as they say, "in the weeds." This is where you do your daily battle.

A Day in the Life

	10 Thursday
9am	**STUDY** Calculus Practice Problem s/ Chapter 12
10:00	**CALCULUS:** Practice Problems Due
11:00	
12pm	
1:00	**STUDY** Read Ch 3 Literature / Start research for paper
2:00	
3:00	**VOLUNTEERS CLUB MEETING**
4:00	**LACROSSE PRACTICE**
5:00	
6:00	
7:00	**STUDY** Read Chem / Do some practice problems / Read History Ch 4
8:00	

Figure 4.4. *Thursday during* Tim's semester

The biggest difference between the weekly and daily schedule is that Tim is now assigning tasks to the study time. He's moved from big-picture strategy onto the playing field where he's executing his plan. If he doesn't finish each of those tasks listed, he will simply add those onto the next day's study schedule. He'll do this every night, and it will only take a minute or two. Tim will also "zoom out" to the weekly and monthly views to glance at the road ahead. Zooming in and out will allow him to strategize his week and semester while simultaneously deciding on his daily tactics. Strategy is for the big picture. Tactics and tasks are for the daily battle. Tim is nailing college and having a blast doing it.

Tracking Your Study Hours Progress

Now that you've learned how to estimate your study hours and use a calendar as a strategic tool, it's time to learn the tremendous value that comes from tracking your study hours. In flight school, I learned that there are two parts to navigation: plotting your course and tracking your progress. Tracking your progress is the only way to predict if you'll reach your destination or goal. (How do you know if you'll reach your destination if you don't know where you are?) Furthermore, it's the only way to know if you're off course, which is also mission-critical information. Remember, grades are not effective for tracking progress. Grades are a result of how you spent your time; they come *too late* to use for time management.

The very best part of logging hours is the motivation it provides. Tracking is the *procrastination buster.* Many students (myself included) found that logging hours became motivating because of how fast those pockets of study time added up. When you take advantage of little pockets of time throughout the day and then get home at night to find out that these pockets added up to a balanced four hours or so of studying, you'll be motivated by the joy that comes with stress-free downtime. At the end of the day, you won't even feel like you did that much. This is a great feeling.

Tracking makes college seem easier than it is because your capacity for learning is maximized. Compare that great feeling to the sinking feeling of getting home and knowing that you have to study for what may be four to six hours. Now try doing that studying while everyone else is watching movies and that guy or girl you like wants to grab coffee. When students make this transition, they literally take off. It's joyous to watch.

In chapter 3, I discussed Craig Alexander and his Iron Man victory. Craig (like all professional athletes) tracks every training session every day. Craig measures how far and fast he swam, ran, or biked that day. He also logs his intervals and his times. Most likely, he has software (and a coach) helping him to analyze his progress so that he can make strategic decisions before the day of the triathlon. Craig wants to understand his progress as soon as possible to be in peak condition on race day. He does *not* want to find out on the big day that he didn't swim enough to succeed. Race day, or even a few days before race day, is *too late* to do anything about a weakness.

The strategic student needs to think the same way. Test day or project due dates are your race day. It's *not* the time to find out you didn't put enough work into certain areas of your studies. You won't have to track to the level of detail that an athlete does, but if you want to succeed in college, you have to track the hours you spend on each subject with just enough detail to maintain balance, and it only takes a minute or so per day. Tracking not only helps you stay balanced, it prevents procrastination. Nothing says you've been ignoring a class like a big goose egg on your study log next to that subject matter.

There's no set format for tracking your study hours, whether you do this on a piece of scrap paper or use a spreadsheet. Both methods have benefits and limitations. Whatever works for you is fine. Just use whatever method is *easiest*. Logging study hours should take around two seconds at the end of each study session.

Using Paper to Track Your Progress

Its benefit is its ease of use. Fold it up, stick it in your bag, and you're good to go. Simply list your classes with study goals (written in hours in parenthesis), and every time you log a session, just jot it down and add up the hours. Table 4.2 shows you how you might format your log using scrap paper.

Table 4.2. Scrap Paper Log Example

	Calculus (9 hours goal)	English Lit (4 hours goal)	Biology (8 hours total: 6 hrs studying + 2 hrs for lab work)	Spanish (3 hours goal)	TOTAL (24 hours)
Sunday					
Monday					
Tuesday					
Wednesday					
Thursday					
Friday					
Saturday					
TOTAL HOURS					

The limitation of using scrap paper is that it's work intensive to roll this view into a big-picture view of the month or semester. For example, it's okay to have an imbalanced week and dedicate a substantial portion of your time to one class. But it's helpful to know how that affects the rest of the month or semester so that you can gain ground the following week. One of my best students kept her log on a napkin from a coffee shop. That was okay by me, because it worked for her. Just remember, *scrap paper gives you only a weekly view.*

Using a Spreadsheet to Track Your Progress

One benefit of using a spreadsheet (like Google Docs) is that you can view a big picture (month or semester), medium picture (weekly), or daily picture. Spreadsheets also allow you to create graphs that allow for quick interpretation of your progress versus your goals. The example shown in figure 4.5 is the type I use. The left bar shows how much the student wants to study, and the right bar shows how much the student has actually studied so far. The limitation of a spreadsheet is that you have to have a computer handy. Furthermore, spreadsheets take a little bit of practice and can seem intimidating at first. But they're easy to use, and I encourage you to try using them.

Study Graph Example

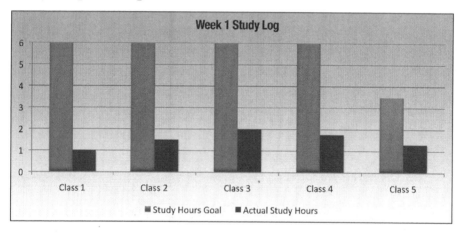

Figure 4.5. *Study graphs compare your goal with your progress.*

A few of my best students logged their hours on paper and then input the hours into a spreadsheet at the end of the day. I used a spreadsheet when I returned to school and found it to be very effective.

Using Your Professor's Time Allocation as a Study Guide

You have learned how to estimate, track, and balance the study hours of your whole schedule, but what about within a single class? How do you determine how much time to spend on each class topic? The simple answer lies with your professor. Your professor will communicate the importance of each topic via the syllabus as well as the time devoted in class to a particular topic. *You're going to mirror your professor's allocation of time.* Let's look at an example to highlight how to mirror your professor's time. Katie is taking Economics 101, and this week, she has her first test, which covers chapters 1 through 4. Katie has already done all of her readings and homework. On Sunday and Monday, she has four hours of studying scheduled for economics. How much time should she spend studying each chapter? Ninety-nine percent of my students answered this question, "One hour per chapter" (4 hours ÷ 4 chapters = 1 hour per chapter). The answer makes sense, right? Not necessarily. This logic assumes that all the chapters are equally important (see figure 4.6). Why would you assume that? If the professor communicates that all the chapters are equally important, that's one thing. But you're a strategic student, so you're not going assume.

Study Time Allotment: Conventional Logic

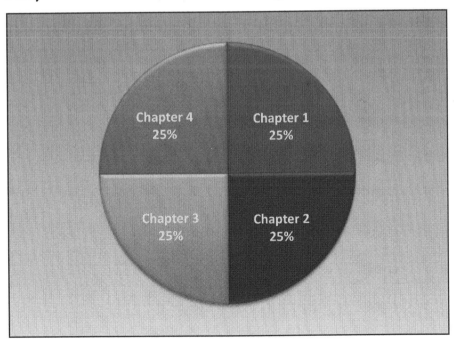

Figure 4.6. *Conventional logic suggests that you spread your study time equally over all chapters that will be on the test. Conventional logic isn't always the best approach.*

Let's say Professor Smith is the Economics 101 teacher, and he covered the four chapters according to the following schedule:

Week 1: Chapter 1

Week 2: Chapters 2 and 3

Week 3: Chapter 4

Week 4: Chapter 4 (continued)

Based on the above schedule, Professor Smith has chosen to allocate his class time as shown in figure 4.7.

Professor Smith's Time Allotment

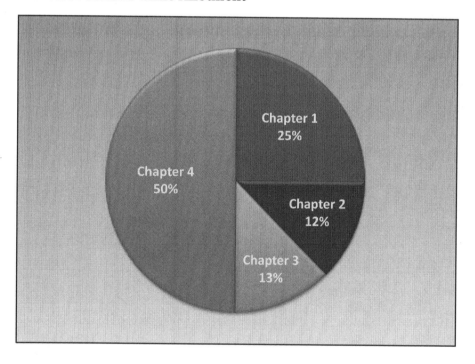

Figure 4.7. *Professor Smith has not given equal attention to the four chapters that will be on the test.*

If Professor Smith chose to spend his valuable class time according to the breakdown shown in figure 4.7, shouldn't you do the same with your study time (at least as a starting point)? Based on Professor Smith's choice, I'd assume one of two things: the test will be divided roughly 25 percent on chapter 1, 25 percent on chapters 2 and 3, and 50 percent on chapter 4, or chapter 4 is the densest, chapter 1 is second, and chapters 2 and 3 are tied for third.

Either way, your study plan should mirror the way your professor's time was committed. So if I were Katie and I was preparing for Professor Smith's econ exam, I'd spend one hour on chapter 1 (25 percent), a half hour each on chapters 2 and 3 (25 percent), and two hours on chapter 4 (50 percent). In other words, I'd mirror the professor. Don't equally distribute your study time if the professor didn't equally distribute the class time. Once you discover topic areas where you're confident, trim the study time spent there and increase it in areas that are more difficult for you.

Right there in black and white, professors will tell you how important class topics are by how much time they're planning to devote to each topic. And now you have your starting point for calculating your study time per class. The question to be constantly asking is, "How much time are the professors spending on each area of study?" At some point, you'll start to instinctively sense these proportions and how important a topic is based on how much class time the professors are devoting to it.

> As a starting point for allocating your study hours within a single class, mirror your professor's time allocation.

Summary

Master time management and you will master college. Time management is so important because it adds a level of structure to an unstructured environment. The military did this for you—which is good because it means you already have the discipline to succeed. The difference is that now you must design and implement the time-management plan yourself. Your school will not teach you these skills, but if you teach yourself, college will seem easier, your

GPA will be higher, and you will be less stressed. Time management can be summarized by four easy steps. Follow these steps, and you will study the right amount and stay balanced throughout the whole semester:

1. Estimate (your goal for study hours per class).
2. Execute (study).
3. Track (your progress against your goals).
4. Repeat (as the semester moves on, refine your study hours goal).

Once you get the hang of tracking your study hours for one semester, you'll never have to think about it again because it is really *easy*. I recommend continuing to read the rest of the book but suggest that you revisit this chapter again when implementing your study plan.

Chapter 5

Classroom Skills: Maximizing the Quality of Your Time with Your Professor

The future belongs to those who prepare for it.
—Ralph Waldo Emerson

As you've read in previous chapters, the vast majority of your learning in college takes place outside of the classroom. Understanding this fact increases the importance of your class time because it's so limited. Great classroom skills are the strategic student's springboard for efficient and productive study time. This chapter will show you how to maximize your in-class learning so that you won't have to study any more than is necessary.

Boost Learning in Class, Reduce Study Time Later

In chapter 4, I outlined a four-step time-management process: estimate—execute—track—repeat. Recall that the reason for the "repeat" step is to let you fine-tune your original estimation. This means you either adjust or not adjust your estimation as your experience in a particular class grows. In other words, you may decrease, increase, or not change your weekly study hours. Ideally, you're either remaining constant or decreasing your original estimation.

To ensure you won't need to increase your study hours, you'll want to make the most of your limited classroom time, which is only about twelve to fifteen hours a week. The following basic strategies will help you squeeze the greatest value out of those short sessions with your professor, thereby enhancing your in-class learning.

1. **Show up—I don't mean just physically.**

When I returned to college as a freshman, I spent time in the classroom studying student behavior. I saw behavior that you would never see in a military classroom. I saw many students texting and surfing the web, and one time, I even saw a student watching a television show on Hulu.com. And don't get me started on Facebook. You're only going to be in class for about an hour; you won't miss anything in that hour, I promise. Showing up simply means shutting down your other media and being present in that class. If you're not there mentally, there's little reason to be there physically.

2. **Learn what you need to learn.**

The job of high school teachers is to teach. In college, your professor's job is partially to teach but mostly to help support your learning. You can't possibly learn all that you need to learn in class alone. I remind you of this because as an advisor, I saw many students who felt defeated or left behind when classes started. Some complained that their professors went too fast and they couldn't mentally keep up. Others got the uncomfortable sense they were slowing their class down when the professor remarked, "We have to move on." Don't worry about this. Classes are designed to move fast and often faster than our minds. Leave each class having learned some material but also with notes on what you need to study. Studying and time management are your equalizers.

3. **Don't sit in the back.**

In every class I taught, the back row was always the first to fill up. I assumed it was me, but the same thing happened in every class I was a student in as well. In the classes I taught, the students who sat closer to the front scored higher grades. I don't believe where you sit determines your grades, though I'm convinced that students who sit up front are more engaged physically and mentally. This is especially true in large lecture halls. It can be very easy for your mind to wander when you're far from the spotlight.

4. **Schedule your classes strategically.**

Give some thought before scheduling your class time. I had a student who scheduled 8:00 a.m. classes and slept through half of them. If you're a morning person, schedule your classes accordingly. If you're not a morning person, don't schedule morning classes. Play to your strengths.

There Most Certainly Are Dumb Questions

I began teaching naval science classes at the University of Colorado on the basis of my navy education and career as an officer rather than being a trained academic, hence the title assistant (or adjunct) professor. My position was to be for three to four years, and I had to learn fast how to be an effective educator and advisor. I'm telling you this because I am not a traditional educator and I view academics with a perspective different from those who have spent their whole careers on campus. I've worked with various professors at the University of Colorado and have had many discussions about education and student mentality. My aim here, and throughout this book, is to provide some insight into how professors think and in so doing help create self-reliant students who strategically navigate their own academics.

We've all heard it said, "There are no dumb questions." I've actually heard professors say it out loud to their classes. Yet some professors have discussed with me the "dumb question(s)" they heard in their classes. I admit—I've heard plenty of dumb questions in my classes, too. I can also tell you that professors will form negative opinions about you based on those dumb questions, which can adversely affect your grades. What exactly constitutes a dumb question? *A dumb question is a question that reveals you did nothing to prepare for the class.* It shows that you chose not to do the assignment. Let me give an example. One day in my navy history class, I was lecturing on the Battle of Tripoli. To prepare the students for the lecture, I assigned them a short chapter about the Barbary Wars, which discussed when the Battle of Tripoli occurred. Here are two dumb questions I received and why I thought they were dumb:

1. "What war was the Battle of Tripoli in?"

While I don't expect students to understand everything they read prior to class (that's why we have class), the student who asked this question would have known what war Tripoli was in if he simply read the first paragraph of the chapter and nothing else. He just conveyed to me he hadn't even glanced at the assigned reading.

2. "Where is the Barbary Coast?"

If the student who asked this question had merely flipped to the chapter opening, she would have seen a map on the second page. She just conveyed to me she didn't even open her book.

The vast majority of questions are *not* dumb. Any question that conveys "I read the chapter but didn't understand [fill in the blank]" is fine. In fact, it's better than fine; by asking engaging questions, you're helping the professor teach the material. Here's an example of such a question: "Why were pirates conducting attacks on American ships off the Barbary Coast?" This question shows you read the chapter but didn't understand something. It will now kick off a great discussion. Teachers love questions, and most of us hate lecturing to silent classes.

In summary, there are dumb questions and professors do make note of them. A dumb question conveys you didn't do the assignment and you didn't even try. If you get behind and miss an assignment from time to time, here's what I would do: sit quietly and take notes. Do not raise your hand and even suggest that you didn't care about your assignment and now want the professor to bring you up to speed at the class's expense.

Recommended Versus Required Reading

There's a difference between recommended reading and required reading. If your professor doesn't explicitly delineate which is which, ask or check with a previous student of the class. Students rarely have time to read everything prior to class—and that's okay. Don't let that crush your spirit. Read it all if you can, but at the very least, read the required portion and you'll be adequately prepared.

Any question that shows you read the assignment but would like clarification is *great* and is never dumb. I think those are the types of questions professors are referring to when they say, "There is no such thing as a dumb question."

> Dumb questions tell your professor you didn't even attempt the assignment.

Participate in Class

On the first day of every class, you'll get a class syllabus that contains lots of great information: class schedule, assignments, honor code guidelines, and the grading system. Find the section titled "Class Participation." Class participation can constitute up to 25 percent of your grade. In other words, it can move you a letter grade up or down, so don't take it lightly.

A common misconception about class participation is that "every student gets an A in class participation." One day, before class, I was setting up my computer and I overheard students in the front row of the class discussing and calculating hypothetical final grades. One student said, "Assuming I get an A in class participation, I'll get a B in this class." He said this right in front of me! I asked him why in the world he would assume an A, and he responded, "I don't know; I guess I just assumed that students get A's in class participation." So I asked the class if they all assumed that class participation was an easy A, and most agreed. The class was mostly freshmen, and I was grateful that one sophomore raised her hand and said, "That is absolutely not true."

Every semester after that incident, I explained to my classes that I didn't give away A's in class participation and that students had to earn them. I also communicated what it takes to earn an A and that I would happily give every one of them an A if they met my criteria. At the end of every semester, I'd have at least one student in my office begging for an A in participation (it was 20 percent of my grade). It was always a student who never spoke up in class and never came prepared. Why on earth would I give that student an A? I couldn't with a clear conscience.

Getting an A in class participation is easy if you do the following:

- **Show up "reasonably" prepared.** I included the word *reasonably* because I understand you can't always complete all of the reading prior to a class. But you can read enough to understand the subject matter and engage in the class discussion.
- **Ask a question**—but not just any random question. Think of something you read and would really like some clarity or perspective on. There's always at least one thing you won't completely understand.
- **Offer an alternative opinion.** In classes that are heavy on debate, such as ethics, history, or political science, the class as a whole will often have a dominant opinion. Offer an alternative view. It adds to the health of a discussion. Let's say you're discussing a difficult and heated issue like the US invasion of Iraq in 2003. The class will likely develop a tilt in one direction or the other in the first few minutes of the discussion. Consider offering an opposing view. Even if you don't agree with the view, you can offer a different perspective. Professors love a healthy debate, and the learning for everyone grows from this type of interaction.
- **Know your professors.** Perhaps I should have said make sure they know you. Your interaction with your professors will be minimal (roughly three hours a week). Introduce yourself at some point. Stop by during their office hours at least once. Professors are human, and connecting with them (without pestering) goes a long

way. (I do not recommend trying to squeeze this in right after class when they're surrounded by a swarm of students.)

- **Share your experience.** As a veteran you have life experiences that your traditional classmates—and likely your professor—cannot comprehend. If you are comfortable doing so, I recommend you share your global experiences when it relates to class discussion. You bring a mature worldview that will enrich the classroom. Your professor and your classmates will likely appreciate your perspective and your leadership. Perhaps more importantly, you will start to see the powerful connection between your military education and your academic work.

Participating in class is easy, and it will serve you well. Not only will it ensure you earn an A in class participation, but you'll be more engaged and consequently learn more. Even if the class doesn't have a class participation grade, the proactive habits you're applying are making you a better student.

Staying Organized Saves Time

Staying organized for each of your classes is crucial because it will cut down on your study time. There are multiple strategies for staying organized, and strategic students will experiment to find what works best for them. When I interviewed students about this subject, I learned that the most successful students had a system of staying organized, though none of the systems were identical in their entirety. The students agreed, however, that having a good system cut down on their study time, which is what all students strive for.

When I returned to school as a freshman, I met with three other students one afternoon at 5:00 p.m. to study Chemistry 101. I watched the other students unload their books and notes. Two of these students shuffled through stacks and laptops and grumbled phrases like, "Does anyone have the handout from last week?" They didn't start actually studying until 5:30 p.m. Being disorganized cost them thirty minutes. That may not sound like much, but let's assume these students are taking multiple classes and they're equally disorganized in those other classes. They're losing around five hours a week to disorganization. This assumption is based on twenty hours of weekly studying split into ten, two-hour sessions. The third student had everything she needed laid out in front of her and started studying right away. This student also left earlier than the others to meet up with friends. Being organized probably saved her five hours a week. If she used that additional time to study, that's a ten-hour difference from her disorganized classmates. What an advantage! And she's going out to have fun while they continue working.

Strategies that help you organize your materials for maximum time efficiency should be personalized to suit you. The following is a discussion of several methods that well-organized and successful students have found helpful.

Organize Materials Chronologically

Every organized student I have ever met arranges materials in the order they are received in class. Human memory typically associates events with other events. It's more common to say something along the lines of, "I remember that concert—it was the night of the Nebraska-Colorado game" than, "I remember that concert—it was October 4." When you keep your materials in order, you won't have any problems finding them because you'll associate the items with a timeframe or another event. If I asked, "Where are those notes Professor Smith gave you the first week of school?" you'd reply, "Right in the first few pages of my notebook," that is, if you organized them chronologically.

Use a Three-Hole Punch and Three-Ring Binder

Most classes still have some paper materials. Paper is easy to organize; all you need is a three-ring binder and a three-hole punch. Every time you get a handout or take notes or receive a graded assignment, date it, punch it, and binder it in chronological order. Three-hole binders are the best because you can insert your graded assignments in the location associated with when you completed them (it may be weeks after you completed an assignment before your professor returns it). You can also put dates on your assignments that you hand in in order to quickly determine a notebook location when the assignment is returned.

If you're using digital files, such as Google Docs, pdf's, or Microsoft Office files for notes and other things, you should organize these chronologically as well. Simply create a class folder and title your files with a date name, such as "01_23_Class Notes.docx." Now you can sort your files to list in chronological order. I use numbered dates instead of month names because month names are not alphabetized, and I want to be able to sort my files to read in order (figure 5.1). Don't depend on the date tags on your computer to organize your files because they update each time you open a file, which can cause lots of confusion.

Sample Class Folder Using Date Tags (PC)

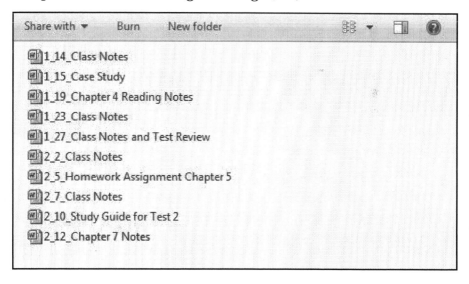

Figure 5.1. *Label* the files in your class folder using numerical date tags, and they display chronologically. This figure shows a class folder with files from January through February. To make sure documents always sort in order, you may want to include leading zeros for the fall semester, e.g.: 09_14, 09_15, 10_02, 11_05, etc.

The Organizer Show

In every class, there are students who offer an Oscar-winning performance about their organization. They have little labeled color-coded tabs hanging out of their books, and they sit down in class with a stack of colored highlighters. They even get there early to "set up." They spend so much time trying to develop an organization masterpiece that learning the material comes second. Organization is not to be overly analyzed. It helps your learning but can never substitute for actually learning.

My experience as a professor taught me that the over-organizers are never the high scorers, and often, they're the low scorers. I mention this because I found that other students can become intimidated by over-organizers or even try to emulate them. Now that you know this, you can sit back and enjoy the show as they rustle through their highlighters in class.

Use Folders

This one is simple. Students who fold up paper documents and stick them in their textbooks are typically disorganized. It makes retrieving the materials needed harder and losing them easier. If you find yourself becoming a giant folder, take stock and work on developing a new method that incorporates chronology for each of your classes.

Organization = Less study time

Let Your Professor Take Your Notes

I almost titled this section "Take as Few Notes as Possible," but I thought that might be misleading even though it's a good goal.

Professors are becoming increasingly technologically savvy, and that means less note-taking for you in class. When I returned to school, I saw many students frantically copying everything the professor had on the board. They were hustling so much that they weren't engaged in the dialogue or even really listening. In most of those classes, the digital notes (such as a Microsoft PowerPoint presentation) had already been posted online by the professor, yet the students still felt compelled to copy them down. What a waste of time and energy.

The following technological platforms are a sample of what professors are using today. Let them work for you. If your professors are not using these items, ask them if they'd be willing to. You'd be surprised what you can get if you just ask.

Slides

Professors who use any kind of slide show presentation (most use Microsoft's PowerPoint) will probably post their presentation on a web-based platform prior to class. Download the file and bring it to class. Take your notes directly in the presentation, or print the presentation before class to take notes on, making sure to leave ample space to write. I like three slides per page because it leaves plenty of room to take notes yet uses minimal paper (figure 5.2).

You're not wasting time regenerating notes that the professor already has on the board; rather, you're augmenting her notes with additional points. Keep in mind that a professor is not going to read you the slides; she's going to talk to the slides. Now you have time to hear what she's saying. (More on note-taking in the next section.)

Taking Notes in Class

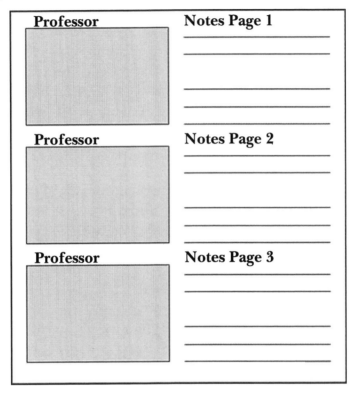

Figure 5.2. Printing your professor's presentation in a three-panel format allows you to simply combine his or her notes with your handwritten notes (in the right column) in class.

Interactive Whiteboards or SMART Boards

Interactive whiteboards are boards professors use to write on directly and save the content into a digital file. Smart Technologies is the name of the company that developed first interactive whiteboards, called SMART Boards, in 1991 (they are not the only producers of interactive whiteboards). The beauty of interactive whiteboards is that professors can save their notes as a pdf file for you to download later. Interactive whiteboards are especially effective in math and science classes where problem solving is part of the instructional methods. You no longer have to race to copy those lengthy math problems your professor writes on the board. He or she can handwrite notes and problem solutions right into their presentation (see sidebar "A Professor's Use of Interactive Whiteboards"). You simply listen in class, jot down some notes, follow along actively, and download the file into a nice study guide. If your professors use interactive whiteboards, take advantage of this technology to make study guides. If they don't use interactive whiteboards, try asking if they'd be willing to.

A Professor's Use of Interactive Whiteboards

The diagram above is of Dr. Mary Mattson's whiteboard from her organic chemistry class at Front Range Community College. The goal this day was to discuss monosaccharides; therefore, Dr. Mattson delivered to her students the presentation notes (the typed slides) before class. She then completed an example problem (the handwritten notes) in class and even noted a textbook page number during her lecture (p. 1034 and figure 27.4) to reference while studying. Dr. Mattson subsequently uploaded notes to the class website to allow students to download in a pdf file for studying. Dr. Mattson is a model example of a professor helping students by embracing technology. Unfortunately, most students still don't take advantage of these amazing study tools. Students would maximize in-class listening if they embrace this use of technology.

iTunes U

Professors have the option to record the audio portions of their class lectures or discussions and post the files on iTunes U. If you miss a class or had trouble keeping up in class, listening to the class again can help you keep up or review. I recommend listening to a lecture while reading along with your class notes if available. You can also add new notes that you may have missed during a difficult lecture series.

Education technology is a growing field, and there are more options beyond what I've listed here. My advice is generic: if professors have a method to capture class content for you, let them. You're fortunate—now you can augment the notes with your own, thereby minimizing how much note-taking you have to do in class. Why use just your brain when you can use your brain and a computer to capture your professor's wisdom?

Note Taking: Digital Versus Handwritten

Note-taking is not a talent; it's a skill that anyone can learn. It's also personal, and no one style will fit everyone's needs, though I have noticed a few commonalities among effective students. The most important theme I've noticed is that effective notetakers generally use two different strategies: one for qualitative classes (digital) and one for quantitative classes (handwritten). Qualitative classes are reading, writing, and discussion orientated. Quantitative classes are math and problem-solving focused. Each type of class requires a distinct strategy and the two strategies can't be used interchangeably. After testing various strategies, I found the following guidelines to work well.

Note-Taking in Qualitative Classes

Qualitative classes are nontechnical; therefore, your notes will stem from verbal discussion. I recommend typing notes in these classes. Any word-processing or note-taking program will do. Some students like OneNote (Microsoft). I personally like Word (Microsoft). Each class will be different in terms of teaching style and content. You'll have to adapt, but the habits described here will help you do that.

So you have your laptop open in class. You've turned off Facebook, Twitter, IM, and other media programs, and your blank document is open and ready to go. Turning off your autoformat will prevent needless automatic editing in class. You are not concerned with spelling and grammar; you are concerned with speed. Therefore auto-formatting cues will be a burden for you in class. You can always turn it back on later.

Professors in almost all qualitative classes lead lectures and discussions with *questions*. They start the class with a question, and they drop questions throughout. These questions aren't random. Your professor has an hour to hit a certain number of topics, and those questions are designed to keep things on track. Every time your professor asks a new question, type it into your computer. Getting the question down is most important. Even if you don't hear the answer, you can always research the answer later or ask the professor during his office hours or in the next class.

Questions are followed by answers, right? True, but in qualitative classes, there often are no right answers. Classes such as political science or literature encourage opinion and debate. You will not be graded on your opinions; you will be graded on your delivery of the evidence you use to support your opinions. So under the question you type, make note of facts that support both sides of an argument. Don't assume you'll be able to choose the side of an argument on a test. You may have to argue multiple perspectives so take notes that include "for," "against," and all other alternative perspectives.

For example, let's say you're in an economics class arguing the virtue of US Treasury Secretary Henry Paulson's Troubled Asset Relief Program (TARP) in October of 2008. The TARP program proposed that the US Treasury would acquire up to seven hundred billion dollars' worth of mortgage-backed securities and is controversial because it represented the US government aiding private banks (who were accused of causing the problem to begin with). A class question may be, "Was the implementation of TARP an effective strategy in the effort to relieve America's recession?" That's a controversial question and one that's difficult to prove either way. There are only two possible answers: yes or no. The answer doesn't matter; the evidence you choose to support your answer is where you make your money (no pun intended).

I like professors. They're the stars of the show. And like most stars, they're often great communicators. They use both verbal and nonverbal language to communicate emotion. As a notetaker, you can use this language as a "giveaway." Many times, professors ask a question and then immediately answer it. That's verbal communication. When a professor asks a question and students answer the question via debates and/or discussion, *notice whether the professor is saying yes or nodding in agreement.* Many students only note what professors say and ignore their classmates' points. In the class I taught, if a student made a key point that I thought that was great, she did my job for me. I'd simply communicate that it was an excellent point. Pay attention to your classmates, and take note of your professor's verbal cues and body language. That's it. Format and style are all subjective to the note-taker.

Professors don't only communicate in class via questions. As a note-taker, you need to capture these themes as well. You can use the same page of notes to capture these points. Keep a keen ear open for your professor stating the following phrases (or similar):

- "It's important to note…"
- "Key point"
- "Very important"

The benefits of typing notes are speed in recording information and ease of editing. The main benefit of speed is that you get more down in less time, thus increasing your listening time. Another benefit of typing is your ability to edit, augment, and organize the material later. Some students like to "tidy up" their notes or even put them into an outline form. With a digital file, you can do this very easily. Handwritten notes are nearly impossible to do this with unless you're willing to spend hours transcribing notes.

Typing also sets you up to make a nice study guide. You're likely going to be taking notes not only in class but also from your book, articles, and perhaps other research. As you get closer to exam time, you merge your notes into one study guide (figure 5.4). With digital files, you can quickly copy and paste notes from multiple sources into one study guide. Don't cut and paste everything—just highlights, key points, and definitions. Organize your notes under common topics. The night before a test, your study guide and practice test(s) (if you have them) are the only things you should be looking at. Can you imagine doing this by hand? Impossible. With a computer, it takes only minutes.

Making Your Study Guide with the "Cut-and-Paste" Function

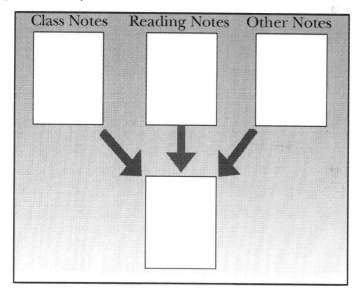

Study Guide

Figure 5.4. Consolidating your notes is very easy when you can "cut and paste" from all of your note-taking resources.

Remember: type your notes. Make note of all questions asked in class, and make note of supporting evidence to those questions (you can do this while studying as well). If you've done the above, you can cut and paste your questions into a study guide. When it comes time to study for your test, all you need to review is your outline and possibly your practice tests. This is your reward for being so organized!

Note-Taking in Quantitative Classes

Taking notes in technical classes that involve mathematical problem solving is much more difficult than in nontechnical classes. I have yet to find a way to avoid writing notes by hand in these classes. The best supplements to handwritten notes are the interactive whiteboard files (usually a pdf file). For now, let's assume that your professor is *not* using an interactive whiteboard. There's no way around it: bring your pencil (not pen) and paper, and be ready to copy sample problems. One reason quantitative classes are so hard to take notes in is because of the symbols used. Numbers, Greek letters, arrows, and lots of steps are the norm in math and science classes. Another reason is that many professors get messy quickly (especially math and science professors). They try to squeeze lots of steps onto a whiteboard or some other similar medium, and it can get chaotic up there.

I recommend two steps for note-taking in these technical problem-solving-type classes. The first step is to *note the subject matter* the problem is testing. For example, let's say you're in physics class and your professor starts the class with the following problem:

A golf ball is moving to the right at 50 m/s, and it strikes another golf ball moving to the left at 75 m/s. Determine speed and direction of both balls after the collision.

Start your note-taking by annotating what subject matter is being tested. In this case, you'd note something along the lines of "Kinetic Energy, Collisions, and/or Conservation of Momentum." Don't worry about filling in notes on that subject in class; you can go back to your book and review theories and take notes. Always know what subject matter a problem is before starting it. This will benefit you tenfold come test time.

The second note-taking step is to *copy practice problem(s)*. Copy problems in steps. Professors often won't write which step they're on while problem solving but will say it. Most students copy only what is on the board. Make note of the steps being completed. This is almost more important than the problem because you can find sample problems later and apply the right steps. Other than that—copy, copy, copy. Get the steps written down even if you don't understand them. Copy now and learn later if necessary. Try to write neatly so that you can redo practice problems later. One of my best students would rewrite the problem neatly right after class while the lessons were fresh. Come test time, he had no problem reviewing. His notes were organized and legible.

So for quantitative classes, there are few shortcuts (which is probably why they have a reputation for being so hard). Your note-taking sets up your studying. Step one is to understand what concepts the problem is addressing. Step two is to apply the correct steps. Following this thought process in your note-taking creates a very effective test-taking thought process. As you can see, you're note-taking with the end goal of easier studying for your test.

I still recommend consolidating notes for quantitative classes, although it is significantly more difficult to do. You can either hand copy notes or scan copies of problems. Hand copying has the benefit of being able to neaten up your notes; however, it is time-consuming. Scanning is fast but you get an exact copy of your notes, which may be messy.

Consolidate Your Notes

The goal of consolidating your notes is to have a concise outline to study in the days prior to your test. During your studies, you'll have information from multiple sources (textbook, class, research, etc.). Consolidating your notes has tremendous benefits, including saving you time. Remember, you're consolidating only the big ideas and important memory items to review, such as a sample problem that's representative of a type of problem your professor uses. Or, maybe you'll list bullet points presenting sides of an argument. The night before an exam, you should *not* be reading chapters or learning any new material. You should be reviewing your outline and perhaps looking at practice tests.

If you've been consolidating notes throughout the semester, your final exam study guide is already made; you just have to put your notes in order. If your professor gives you a list of final exam topics to focus on, all you have to do is cut and paste your notes about those items from your earlier outlines that semester and you'll be ready to study the material in a focused and organized manner.

What to do When You Don't Have a Great Professor

It's inevitable that at some point you will have a class taught by a professor who is simply not an effective teacher. So how do you handle this? Many students become angry and openly criticize the professor's shortcomings. This approach will get you nowhere because your GPA will never have footnotes explaining that you had a few bad professors. You are still responsible for your GPA, and you can't share it with your professors.

Strategic students adapt and overcome a poor professor. They develop a new plan and move forward without wasting any time blaming. The first step is to identify what is missing in the professor. The second step is to fill in the shortcoming with a secondary resource. For example, I had one student, Eric, who said to me, "My calculus professor doesn't assign any homework, so the class doesn't know what type of problems will be on the test." Not assigning homework problems that guide the students' studying was a shortcoming for this particular professor. The passive student will take that methodology to mean that he doesn't have any homework, and his test results will be negative. A strategic student will acknowledge the shortcoming and then take action.

In this particular situation, Eric went to the professor's office hours with his book open and said, "Would you mind circling problems that you think would be good to practice?" The professor agreed, and now Eric had a problem set that the rest of the class did not. Eric also went a step further; he went to another calculus professor's office hours, asked the same question, and further increased his practice problem set. Eric wasn't getting the homework he needed, so he went out and got it for himself. Strategic students always find a way to overcome obstacles. They never accept defeat, and they know that they alone own their GPA.

Summary

Effective in-class habits eliminate unnecessary study time. Class time in college is *not* where most of your learning takes place. This is the biggest academic difference from high school and military learning. In class, remind yourself that you're learning what you need to learn. This theme will help you streamline your note-taking and organizational methods so that studying for exams will be easier and more effective. Working smarter, not harder, is the goal.

Your professor will deliver a one-size-fits-all message because he or she is teaching the class as a whole and not any one individual. Knowing this will allow you to strategically receive and customize that message as a foundation for your study time. So many factors affect the quality of your class time: time of day, seating location, note-taking, and technology to name a few. The good news is that you can control most of these factors and maximize your learning by employing the strategies discussed in this chapter. While your professor is delivering one message to the class, the individuals in the class are not receiving the message equally. Reception has nothing to do with mental aptitude; it has everything to with setting yourself up to effectively receive and organize the inbound information to utilize in your study sessions.

Chapter 6

Study Skills: Mastering Learning Outside of the Classroom

Learning is like rowing upstream:
Not to advance is to drop back.
—Chinese Proverb

In the last chapter, you learned the importance of skills in the classroom. Those skills build the foundation for your study time. Studying outside of class and time management account for the majority of your collegiate learning, and yet your school will not teach you how to study or form a strategy; this chapter will teach those skills. In high school and military classrooms, the "quick students" may have scored the best grades. But in college, the best studiers and time managers are more likely to succeed. Time management, classroom skills, and study skills are the three core areas of expertise you'll need in college to achieve your academic goals. This chapter is dedicated to the study skills I have found to be most powerful. Decide which skills work for you and which don't. Just remember to keep tracking your progress (study hours) to ensure you're hitting your goals.

The Blueprint Approach to Studying for Exams

A blueprint to a house shows the foundation and framework for the home—the big picture. It doesn't show the carpeting, paint colors, or furniture. The foundation and framework need to be in place before the other details are added. Effective studiers follow a similar approach: key points, or big ideas, are your framework, and the details get filled in later. A common mistake that college freshmen make is to drudge through details page by page, learning every item prior to moving forward. You simply don't have enough time for this type of approach, nor is it effective.

Outlines are your blueprints, and they can be found everywhere. They're in your textbooks at the beginning and/or end of each chapter. In fact, the structure of a chapter itself is like an outline—look for section headings as indicators of important concepts. Even your professors communicate using outlines via their syllabuses, slides, and lectures. Class time is the ultimate outline; limited class time means the professor will discuss key points. Learn these key points first and details subsequently (see figure 6.1). Remember, build the house first and decorate it last.

Strategic Approach to Studying

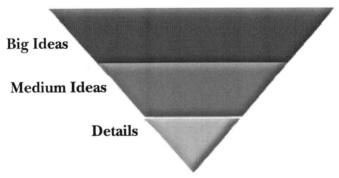

Figure 6.1. Study big ideas (core concepts) first and subsequently learn details (facts, evidence, etc.)

Study Key Points (Big Ideas) First

Studying key points or big ideas first is a damage-control technique. By learning the "big ideas" first, "medium ideas" second, and "details" last, you're setting yourself up for success. If adversity strikes and you run out of study time, you can still do very well and even figure out details during the test.

While studying, think about how long the test will be. Is the test an hour? Two hours? Twenty minutes? How much information could possibly fit into that time frame? (Tests won't cover everything in the assigned readings.) If you were the professor, what would you choose to fit into this time frame? Most professors aren't random in their testing, so with a little thought, you can (and should) predict what will be on the test. Try to think like your professor.

History classes serve as perfect examples for blueprint studying. Let's say you're studying the Civil War. The big ideas to study would be: Who was involved in the war? Why were they involved? What was the result of the war? Medium ideas to study would be: What were the major battles during this war? Who won these battles? What were the effects of each battle? Details would be the names, locations, and specific events that took place within each battle.

Find Out Who Writes the Exams

On the first day of class, the professor goes over the syllabus and often mentions who writes the class's exams. If the professor doesn't tell you who writes the exams and it's not mentioned in the syllabus, I believe the most important question you can ask in any college class is: "Who writes the exams?" The answer to this question tells you what types of study strategies you'll need.

The most common answers fall into three categories:

1. The professor writes the exams.
2. The textbook company generates the exams.
3. The department writes the exams.

In the military, an intelligence team will study the enemy in depth prior to war. They will look at geography, capabilities, strengths, weaknesses, and prior engagements that our enemy has been part of. The role of military intelligence is to provide the military forces with actionable information so that we can prepare an appropriate strategy and train efficiently. Knowing who writes your exams provides you with the exact same value. Understand the challenges ahead, and you can face them more efficiently. Your professor is certainly not your enemy, but the test is, and you are planning to defeat it, right? Your study plan's effectiveness determines your grades. Grades determine your competitiveness for graduate school, a job, and so on. That GPA has a nasty way of following you around for a very long time. Each of the different types of exams has advantages and disadvantages. I do not believe any exam means working more or less, just differently. In the following sections, we'll look at how preparation strategies change depending on who writes the exams. *The main difference between strategizing for each of the three exam types is deciding what your primary study sources are.* You'll be saturated with information via textbooks, notes, study guides, solution manuals, the Internet, and more, and you can't study it all. Your time is limited, so knowing what sources to focus on is crucial.

Study strategies help you manage your limited time, improve your test-taking skills, relieve stress, and ultimately land you a better grade. There is no substitute for learning the material, but study strategies will help you focus your learning with laser precision for test-taking effectiveness.

As you've heard me say before, success in college academics is mostly what you do outside of the classroom. Yet I've been unable to find any class syllabus that offers a study plan. Ultimately, creating a study plan is the student's job. That said, I've never heard of any professor who was unwilling to answer the question, "Who writes the exams?" In fact, a few of my students who asked this question said their professors were impressed that they were thinking this strategically—and on day one of the semester!

Develop an Exam Study Plan

Professor-Written Exams

Professor-written exams are the best. Professors want you to succeed. They are educators, and the vast majority of them care about students and delivering high-quality learning. Don't assume, though, that because they want you to succeed, they have ample time to help you succeed. One-on-one time with a professor will be limited no matter how small your school is. The professor's job is to teach the class as a whole. It's your job to own your academic success.

When professors write their own exams, they teach with the particular exam in mind. Being good educators, they'll tell you in class what's most important to learn. The types of questions they ask in class are the types of question that will appear on the exam. The subject matter they focus on in class will be the subject matter that the exam focuses on. Professors may not tell you explicitly what's on the exam (some professors will), but if you know they're the exam writer and you're constantly thinking along these lines, you won't be shocked when the exam lands in front of you. The best part about professor-written exams is there are few surprises.

With professor-written exams, missing a class, even for a valid reason, really hurts. Every class will communicate a theme and focus that may not be mirrored by the textbook. The wisdom is not just in the professor's notes for the class (discussed in the next section); it's in hearing the professor speak and listening carefully to what's being emphasized. To be successful with this format, you have to be a good notetaker. Chapter 5 provided tips on how to take effective notes.

Study Strategies for Professor-Written Exams
* Most professors who write exams use lecture notes or slides as an outline. Ask professors for their teaching notes or slides (usually on PowerPoint). Many professors post their notes via the school's online portal. *This*

is their road map for teaching, and now it is your outline for studying. These notes will target the most important things you need to learn. It's admirable to try to learn every possible subject in your textbook, but it won't help you focus on the test material. If the professor does not provide notes, your note-taking skills just became even more critical.

- If the professor uses slides, do not study any material that is not addressed on at least one slide until you've mastered the material specifically presented. You certainly need to dive deeper into the subjects mentioned on the slides via the textbook, notes, research, and discussion, but don't drift away from the material listed on the slides. The goal here is to prevent what I call "information chasing." Information chasing is similar to surfing the Internet and getting lost or distracted (as when you get on the web to research a book and an hour has gone by and you're watching a golden retriever dancing on YouTube and don't know how you got there). There's going to be so much information via the textbook and Internet that you could spend many hours chasing questions that arise in your studies.

- Master first what you can expect on the test. I don't like saying it, but I'm recommending you contain your intellectual curiosity—at least until after you've mastered the professor's plan. If your thirst for knowledge is still truly unquenched, then I think you've found your passion and perhaps what your PhD should be in! Don't deviate from the professor's path; it's like having the other team's playbook. A test question outside of the notes is not impossible, but there will be very few.

- Each time the professor asks a question in class, create an internal alert. An internal alert is anything that smacks you in the head. I like to imagine a bell sound followed by the phrase "*Test question—Test question—Test question.*" Do this silently for a week, and you'll start to see a theme developing.

> Lecture notes and outlines (written by the professor) are the most important sources to study for professor-written exams.

Professor-written exams are the best because they are the easiest to create a study plan for. Your professor is telling you every class day what's important—what subject matter you need to learn and what types of test questions will be asked, even the format of the test questions. You just need to know what to listen for.

Textbook Exams

Textbook exams (TEs) are often used in math and science classes, where the information presented is nearly the same at every school. *The primary study sources for TEs are the textbook and supporting materials* from study guides (from the same publisher as the book), online quizzes, tutorials, and so on.

I don't advocate missing classes, but if you must miss a class for which the exams will be textbook generated, it won't kill you. In-class note-taking can be less detailed than in classes where you'll have professor- or department-written exams. Because the textbook company generates the exams, you have all the information you need within their materials. Your primary focus is the textbook and supporting materials, and you have access to that anywhere, anytime!

Although you have all the answers at your fingertips, there's generally a much broader spectrum of material to study than when the professor writes the exams. There are often surprises on TEs. It's very possible to be tested on some detail the book mentions that the professor did not.

Study Strategies for Textbook Exams

- While taking notes in class, don't worry about writing down everything the professor states on a subject. Instead, just make a note of the subject mentioned. Later on, return to that subject and fill in notes based on what the textbook says. Here's an example: your biology professor lectures on Darwin's theory of natural selection. In class, make a note that your professor finds this subject important. Write in your notes something like "Darwin/Natural Selection," and then listen intently to the professor. Fill in your notes under "Natural Selection" later using the verbiage from the authors of the book. The manner that a subject appears in the book is the manner that it will appear on the test. In other words, the test will reflect the author's verbiage, not the professor's.

- Find the textbook's additional resources (even if the class doesn't require you to). Study guides and the supporting website are amazing. These resources often have notes and practice quizzes/tests, which will have a similar tone and level of difficulty that you'll likely see on the test. Your professor may not ever mention these resources, and most students will ignore them, but they are worth their weight in gold come test time.

- Be an active reader. I'm not going to recommend a specific system of note-taking; I will say you need a system. Different methods work for different students. Just make sure that you're being consistent and noting the author's questions that she raises in the context of the book.

Textbook-generated exams can be tough because everything in the assigned reading is fair game. Even that one little sentence mentioning a barely memorable fact may turn up on the test. The good news is that you have your main study source at all times. Remember to tune yourself into the textbook author's tone more so than your professor's. That doesn't mean you ignore your professor, though; your professor is an invaluable resource in explaining subject matter that can be difficult to learn simply by reading and practicing problems on your own.

> The textbook and supporting materials (study guide, website, practice quizzes, etc.) are your main study sources for textbook exams.

Department Exams

A few departments on campus offer many sections of one class. Math classes are a good example. A typical college will generally offer many sections of Calculus 101 or Statistics 101 (to name a few). Sometimes in an effort to standardize the syllabi, the department will gather together the respective professors and they'll write an exam as a team. Some departments do this for every test, and others do it just for the final exam. Either way, you'll need to adjust your study strategy. Knowing how to tailor your study plan based on the type of test will make you a more confident and prepared student and therefore more likely to score high grades.

Department exams are usually written at the start of the semester. Therefore, your professor is likely teaching with the test in mind. This is good because the same strategies I outlined with professor-written exams apply. Remember, for professor-written exams, class notes and outlines are your primary sources of study.

Department exams are also probably the most challenging because they require some extra legwork on your part, which I'll discuss in the following study strategies section. They're similar to professor-written exams with one noteworthy exception: multiple professors are writing the exam. This means you'll likely see various styles and tones on the exam. The types of exam questions may also differ from both the textbook and your professor. Even in standardized courses, some professors emphasize different subjects. If one professor writes a greater portion of the exam, you may find that the exam has more questions on one subject than you feel was emphasized in your class.

Study Strategies for Departmental Exams

- *The biggest difference in studying for department exams is not the study source—it's in your time allocation.* You have to give equal study time to all subject matter even if your professor did not. In other words, while all the professors are teaching the same course, their time (and possibly excitement) per subject matter may differ. You must take an egalitarian approach to subject matter when studying. Let's say you're taking Physics 101 and the department is writing your final exam. One of the professors likes theoretical questions about Newton's laws. Another professor prefers math problems. You need to practice both equally, whereas if Professor 1 was the sole author of the exam, you'd focus much more on theoretical problems.

- Find out who the other professors are and their office hours. This information is generally available on the department's website. Make an appointment or drop by during office hours, and ask the professors what subjects and types of exam problems they emphasize. Here's one way you might frame your question: "Professor Smith, my name is Dave and I'm in another section of Chemistry 101. I'm currently preparing for the next test and would like to ask what subject matter you think I should emphasize while studying. Do you have a few minutes?" Most professors will give you advice in the order of importance, so write down the subjects in the order given. These appointments should take only a few minutes per professor, but you'll need to plan ahead. Gather the information you need from the professors other than your own, and you'll have yourself a clean and concise study guide.

- Another strategy for preparing for department exams is to create a study group with students in the other class sections. This could be challenging because you may not know students in the other classes. Here's how one of my student's did this: Mark discussed the idea of an "intersection" study group with his biology professor. That professor not only communicated the idea to the other classes, but she was nice enough to facilitate a classroom one night a week for the group to meet.

It's truly amazing how much professors and staff will help if you simply ask for it. By the way, the professor was very impressed with Mark's proactive nature, so in one strategic move, Mark created a time-saving study group and impressed his professor. Do you think that at the end of the semester, if Mark's grade is on the fence, the professor will help him push it over? If I were his professor, I would.

Your primary study sources are the same as with professor-written exams: teaching notes and class outlines. Your study time allocation is weighted equally for all the subjects expected to appear on the exam. The only exception to that rule is if all the professors tell you they emphasize the same material in the same order. In that case, you can adjust to meet their priorities.

> Class notes and secondary research (gathered from other professors) are your primary study sources for department exams.

Using Practice Tests

One of the most effective forms of studying is the use of practice tests. Practice tests are either tests the professor gave a previous semester or a sampling of questions from the textbook authors. Most of the students I interviewed over the years used practice tests, and almost all of them said they were very helpful; that's the good news. The bad news is that most students did not use them as effectively or efficiently as they could have. By "efficiently," I mean that the goal is to maximize test preparation in the least amount of time. A criticism I received once from a student was, "It sounds like you're advising me to do the least amount of work." I told him, "Yeah, kind of. I'm trying to get you to do more work in less time."

You're not rewarded for quantity of hours studying alone. You are, however, rewarded for the quantity of correct answers you put on your test. Doing more quality work in less time means you free up time for reviewing more material, studying other classes, exercising, or exploring your new college town.

The best way to use practice tests is to bookend your test preparation time with the tests. Test preparation begins when you're up-to-date on all your reading and you've made it (at least once) through all the material that will be on the test. Start your test preparation with a practice test, and end your studying with a different practice test (or the same one if that's all you have). For each practice test, your goals and execution are different.

Pre-study Practice Test

Move through this practice test, and don't worry about time. Go as slowly as you like. *This first test will identify your areas of strengths and weaknesses* and help determine how you allocate the rest of your study time: more time for weaknesses and less time for strengths. This may seem obvious, but it's human nature to spend more time on what we're good at (you need to resist this temptation).

The test format will vary depending on the type of class. Whether the format involves multiple choice, short answer, essay, true/false, and/or fill-in-the-blank, answer only the questions you know with 100 percent confidence. In other words, *do not guess* (not even a little) on any answers. The danger of guessing during this practice test is guessing correctly. You may be wondering, "What's wrong with guessing correctly? That would mean more points on the test, right?" True, but this is your first practice test. The danger in answering a question correctly after guessing is that it hides the fact that you really don't know that material. It gives you false confidence in the subject matter, and you're likely to ignore that material during your studying.

Try this instead: don't answer the question, but mark it with a question mark. This will be your reminder to include this material on a "to study" list. For essay-type questions, jot a list of talking points. Don't waste time writing out sentences; simply test your ability to produce talking points. If you can't produce the appropriate amount of talking points, mark that question with a question mark. When you're finished with the test, make a list of your highlighted material and get to studying. *In general, on the first practice test, your goal is to distinguish between just getting the right answer and understanding the material behind the question.*

Post-study Practice Test

You're done with studying or close to being done, and you've focused on the items you struggled with on the first practice test. Now you want to practice test taking. *This second test is to practice answering questions at the pace you expect to on the real test.* This test should build confidence and reveal any areas for last-minute review.

One of the biggest pitfalls I've seen students face during tests is summed up with this common phrase: "I understood the material, but I ran out of time." I don't want to sound harsh but too bad. Can you imagine if a basketball coach said, "We could have won if we had more time to score points?"

A vital strategy to master in test-taking is timing. *The pos-tstudy practice test is all about moving with the right combination of speed and accuracy, and that takes practice.* Your professor will have told you the amount of time you'll have for the test as well as the test format (the approximate number of questions and types of questions). So before taking the post-study practice test, divide the class time by the number of questions. This will give you the average amount of time to spend on each question. Practice answering questions in this period of time.

Answer every question. If you don't know the answer, do your best to eliminate wrong answers and then guess. For tests with various sections (e.g., multiple choice, essay, and short answer), take an educated guess on the amount of time per section that you'll need on test day and practice accordingly. After you've scored the test, do a quick review of any material that you've just realized needs a little more attention.

Standardized-test-preparation companies, such as Princeton Review and Kaplan, have been teaching timing for years. Timing is a skill that is certainly not exclusive to the SAT or ACT. Use it for every test to save you time and increase your effectiveness!

Knowledge gained + test-taking skills = GPA

The Power and Pitfalls of Study Groups

Study groups can be very beneficial for college students. One insight from my research that surprised me, though, was how sparingly my top students participated in study groups. When I returned to school and joined a few study groups myself, I learned why. Study groups are promoted by schools because they work in theory but not so much in practice. Most groups are terribly inefficient, and top students know to avoid inefficiency. In fact, groups that aren't well thought out or are poorly run can actually hurt students' grades. If you're thinking of organizing a study group or joining one, the following tips will help you both avoid some of the pitfalls and maximize your involvement.

Criteria for Effective Study Groups

Study groups can be remarkably effective *if and only if* they meet at least three of the following criteria:

- The group consists of like-minded students.
- Members follow specific agendas and topics.
- The format includes teaching.
- Members shouldn't be your friends.

Like-Minded Students

When you're in a group of like-minded students, you're studying with students who move at about the same pace and prefer the same format of studying. Let's start with pace. If one student is moving much faster or slower than the whole group, it just doesn't work. (Ever go jogging with someone who runs much faster or slower than you? You usually end up separating, which was not the point.) As for studying in a similar format, if one student wants to have a discussion, another student wants to work problems on a whiteboard, and yet a third student prefers reviewing notes, it doesn't work because individual preferences are conflicting. And if the group tries to do all three, you're compromising your time. The group must be united in pace and format to be worthwhile.

Specific Agenda Topics

Study groups are most effective when they cover specific topics within a class. For example, meeting to study periodic table trends and solubility problems for a chemistry class, rather than to discuss chemistry in general is more specific and thus more productive. To be efficient at studying, you need to hit the areas that you need to hit. Naturally, students in a group often differ on which topics they individually need to study. So what happens when four students meet and haven't agreed on topics? They spend their precious time compromising. Compromising means more study hours for you. You don't want that. Your goal is to work smarter, not harder.

The Format Includes Teaching

The very best study groups involve teaching, where each student teaches the others at some point. Teaching helps everyone. One of the best ways to test if you understand a concept is to try to articulate it to another person; therefore, the teacher is gaining benefit. An excellent way to gain understanding of a topic you're struggling with is to hear it explained differently. Thus, hearing a topic explained by your peers helps you learn. Everybody wins.

Make sure there isn't just one teacher emerging in the group though; share the duty, and teach each other.

Members Shouldn't Be Your Friends

Friends are your worst study partners. I'd prefer you study with your enemies—at least then you might stick to a topic. I truly believe you're kidding yourself if you try to convince yourself that you can group study with your friends. Would you rather study for two hours alone and then socialize for two hours with your friends or study for four hours with your friends, get very little done, and not really be having fun either? It's win-win or lose-lose, depending on your choice.

How to Use Study Groups

The reason why great students don't study much in groups is because it's hard to meet the criteria mentioned above. Most students create study groups with their friends or with whoever happens to be sitting by them in class. They then meet and end up discussing grades, the last test, the professor's armpit stains, and other such topics. Many groups also end up as a forum for comments like: "I think this test is going to be sooo hard. I am stressed. Are you stressed?" That road ends nowhere, and now you're in a therapy group, not a study group.

If you *can* meet the above criteria (at least three), then you have something powerful and your meetings will benefit the whole team. That said, *I recommend a rough split of 25 percent group study to 75 percent solo study as a general rule.* Like any rule of thumb, it can be adjusted to suit a particular type of class. A class that relies heavily on debate and discussion can benefit more from group study, whereas a math/science class requires less discussion and more head-down-in-the-book type of learning.

My advice is to use study groups but use them lightly because ultimately the majority of the work always comes back to you; this is what I mean by taking ownership of your GPA, time, and education. Moreover, each member must contribute something of equal or greater value or risk being seen as a freeloader. Study groups are not a place to feel out one's classmates for their knowledge levels. Your mission is to partake in or lead well-executed study groups, and run—no, *sprint* from the others.

> Don't use study groups for more than 25 percent of your studying time.

Study Groups Versus Collaborative Groups

A *study group* is a collection of students discussing, processing, and learning material that each student will be tested on individually. A *collaborative group* is a collective effort that will culminate in the delivery of a single assignment by the whole team. Collaborative groups are great for exchanging ideas, debating, or innovating. Examples of collaborative assignments are group presentations, projects, or even a lab exercise. You can delegate responsibilities in a collaborative group; you can't delegate in a study group.

Before meeting with your group, make sure you understand the group's goals. If you don't understand the goals, assume a leadership role and assign a few objectives for reaching those goals. In a collaborative group, if objectives aren't clearly defined and nobody is driving, it will turn into wasted time filled with chatting, arguing, and little accomplishment.

You should leave a collaborative group meeting feeling that you made progress on an assignment. You should leave a study group meeting feeling like you better understand a particular set of material. Understanding the objectives of each group will help avoid the common pitfalls of group work in college. *The key to successful groups is not simply creating them but effectively managing objectives.*

Working with Tutors

I'm a big fan of tutors. Meeting with a tutor is like a study group with a partner who's really knowledgeable and will study exactly what you want. In my ROTC department at the University of Colorado, we hired a math tutor because calculus was a class students commonly struggled with. I interviewed the tutor one day and discovered two problems with the way students utilized this great resource. First, when students make an appointment with a tutor, they often don't realize that the time with the tutor is very limited. Consequently, they may feel cheated when the tutor has to cut them off. Second, when students don't bring specific questions to the appointment, the tutor spends precious time trying to discover the problem areas rather than solving them.

The solution is simple and similar to how you run an efficient study group: be very specific when you meet. Don't just say, "I'm having trouble with these problems." Say, "On problem number 3, I understand how to get to this step, but this is where I get lost." That way, you've pinpointed where you struggle and now the tutor can spend the time helping you overcome your problem area.

> Maximize your time with a tutor by bringing very specific questions to your appointment.

Assign Your Own Homework

Unlike in high school, in college, you'll only turn in papers and major projects; daily or even weekly turn-ins will not be the norm. Professors will provide homework guidelines, though, for chapters to read or a series of problems to solve. While I certainly recommend that you do the work, I don't necessarily think you should do the work as assigned. I recommend you *assign your own customized homework to address your weaknesses.*

Your professors probably don't know you personally. They don't know your strengths and weaknesses; thus, the homework advice they give isn't necessarily designed for you. Strategic students realize this and adjust accordingly.

Let's say you're taking Statistics 101. It's likely to be a large class, so your professor won't collect homework. She will, however, assign problems that she thinks well represents the material that will appear on the test, say probability, normal distributions, and regressions. You have previously concluded you're great at distribution problems, mediocre at regression problems, and terrible at probability problems. As a strategic student, you decide to do less than what's assigned for distribution problems, more than what's assigned for probability problems, and precisely what's assigned for the regression problems. Your time is much more effectively spent if you customize your education to suit your needs. *The fact that most of the learning in college takes place outside of class means you can (and should) customize the learning to address your weaknesses.*

Four Great Study Habits

After a few years of advising, I began to hear about recurring, positive study habits from my very successful students. After I heard a method more than once, I started to share it with other students. When I returned to school myself, I tested out these strategies. This section discusses four of the easiest yet most powerful study habits to help you maximize your academic prowess.

1. Study Where They're Not

One evening, I drove by the engineering building and I saw a student of mine (Frank) walking out. I thought it was kind of odd. The reason I thought it was odd was because Frank was a finance major. I asked Frank the next day why was he was in the engineering building when he goes to the business school. He answered, "That is precisely why." Frank was studying where his buddies were not and where he would not be interrupted. I thought this habit exhibited simple brilliance because Frank knew he'd be tempted if he studied in the business school. Sometimes I see students studying in the veterans' center; this can be a risky endeavor for the same reason Frank avoided the business school: your buddies are there. Buddies are great for camaraderie but not always the best for studying.

2. Study in Intervals

Strategic students study in intervals. Intervals are any amount of time between fifteen minutes and two hours. Another way of putting this is to say that *you don't need to endure long study sessions.* Shorter intervals that add up are the key to studying, and they produce outstanding benefits.

Picture yourself walking into a study room knowing you have four hours of studying to do. The idea of a long study session ahead of you already makes you feel defeated and depressed. This is a bad mind-set for learning. Now picture yourself walking into a study room and you only have one hour of studying to knock out. You're focused and positive. One hour is no big deal, and it will be easy to focus for that amount of time. This is the positive mind-set that results from interval studying.

Ships are built into compartments so that if one section of the ship is damaged, the flooding can be sealed off and the ship will still be operational. When you schedule intervals of studying, it's like building compartments. If one compartment is damaged, it will be isolated and won't infect the rest of the plan.

Let's say you're planning a short, one-hour study session between classes. As you're walking by a quad, you see your friends playing dodge ball. They've already spotted you; how can you resist? You can't, so you join them and don't study. But you've only lost an hour off your master study plan. Scheduling intervals limits your loss. If you had put off studying and were on your way to a needed four-hour session, this dodge-ball game could grow and now your plan is significantly damaged, perhaps even beyond repair.

In summary, never plan for long study sessions. Plan your intervals and track your progress. You'll be surprised how quickly they add up, how focused you'll be, and how little damage is done when something comes up (because it will).

The Power of Fifteen Minutes

Students often ask, "How long does an interval have to be to be effective?" I've experimented with this and interviewed students, and I have found that fifteen minutes is a nice minimum. Some students think nothing can get done in fifteen minutes so they ignore these pockets of time. Average students think an hour of studying is necessary to begin. Great students know that four pockets of fifteen minutes are actually more effective and much less painful than a full hour. They really do add up!

While fifteen-minute intervals can be powerful, they're not appropriate for the type of studying that involves problem solving or group work. Those sessions take a few minutes just to open up your notes and material, and you need longer to get into a groove.

Fifteen minutes is useful for any studying that involves memorizing and reading. Most classes have at least some degree of either. Keep a notecard, a mobile file, or even a single sheet of notes handy. Anytime you have fifteen minutes, pull out your notes and do some reviewing. When you settle in to study that material later, the tedious memorizing work is done.

Mike's Use of Fifteen Minutes

I had a student, Mike, who swore by this technique in foreign language classes. He said he never sat down and studied for Spanish. Instead, Mike crammed some notes daily into his bag and reviewed them whenever he had a pocket of time. Mike got all A's in Spanish and went on to study international business.

Fifteen minutes really helps with reading dense material. Keep your book handy and knock out a few pages at a time. Your mind won't wander, and you can eliminate long sessions of mind-numbing reading. Staring at complex material for many hours at a time is difficult to do, and the material is even more difficult to absorb. Cater to your short attention span; even better—make it work for you as a strategic weapon!

3. Switch It Up

If you start an exercise regimen with a personal trainer or follow the advice of a conditioning coach, they'll change your exercise routine often. Trainers do this because they don't want your muscles to adapt to your current routine, at which point you gain less from your workout session. Your brain is the same way and can "tune out" if it's not continuously stimulated. "Switch it up" refers to the material you're studying at any one session. Excellent students kept telling me that mixing up their study material helped them learn more, and to be honest, I didn't buy it until I tried it myself. Now, I'm a believer. Let's say Lindsay has a two-hour study session scheduled. She knows not to schedule more than two hours but wants to get maximum benefit from her two-hour commitment. If Lindsay isn't efficient, she may get less than two hours of value out of her session and would have to study more later. So she decides to study chemistry for one hour, take a short break to walk around, and then read for her literature class for the second hour. Lindsay's plan is an excellent way to stay mentally engaged and learn more. And learning more is the ultimate goal. It's tough to focus for a long period of time, no matter how interested you are in a subject. When you switch up material, you reengage your brain and you're ready to absorb.

Switching material has the added benefit of helping you maintain balance in your classes. While not every class requires the same amount of study hours, they all do require attention. If you're switching up your material and tracking your hours, you'll strike a balance more quickly, which will help you keep on track in all of your classes.

4. Limit Procrastination

We all know that procrastination can destroy your chances of succeeding academically. It's the dominant reason your classmates pull all-nighters and perform horribly. Not only is it bad for learning, it increases your stress levels. If you decide not to study in order to see a local band play, you probably tell yourself it will be a nice stress reliever. The fact is, you'll be thinking about what you should be doing, so the feeling of procrastination causes you more stress. Seeing the band has now had the opposite effect that you intended. If, on the other hand, you check your study tracker and you're right where you want to be, you go can out, have fun, and not worry about academics. That is a true stress reliever.

Scheduling your study hours first and filling those hours with tasks second is designed to defeat procrastination. Many of my students resisted tracking study hours at first because it sounded like a chore, even though it takes only a minute or so a day. Yet, once they started tracking, they all responded, "Tracking helps me resist procrastinating." Tracking acts as a daily reminder of where you need to be.

When the little voice in your head says, "You need to study [fill in class]," but you rationalize why studying can wait; that's the procrastination train getting started. The earlier you stop that train, the better. If the train gets moving, the next phase is, "I have so much to do, and I don't even know where to start." Do this: go to your syllabus and start wherever you last left off. Starting anywhere is better than not starting at all.

Procrastination will never be eliminated 100 percent, and we're all guilty of it. When it happens, learn to give yourself a break. Simply identify it, stop it, and move on. Pick yourself up, dust yourself off, and get back in the fight. Start tracking again and see how quickly you catch up. You can even add hours to your goals to catch up. Remember, a 4.0 GPA doesn't represent perfection—you only need a 93 percent. You have room for error in college, but not much, so stay balanced in your weekly efforts and you'll limit your procrastination to a minimum.

Summary

Developing and applying effective study skills early and independently is so important because your school will not teach them to you. Furthermore, most of your learning will be spent studying outside of the classroom. Learning to study by trial and error takes too much time and causes too much damage to your GPA. Like most habits in this book, study skills are designed to save you time and reduce stress by getting you to maximize the quality of each study hour. When you maximize the quality of each study hour, you minimize your total time spent studying. And now that you've learned how to allocate time and study effectively, you must learn how to strategically approach test taking, which just so happens to be the subject of the next chapter.

Chapter 7

Test-Taking Skills: Executing on Test Day

Whether you think you can or think you can't; you're right.
—Henry Ford

There are various types of tests you'll encounter during your academic career; almost all of them will look different than tests you took in the military. Military tests were often the start of your training, and instructors often ensured you passed in order to get to the hands-on training. College is very different in that you will you need to apply your knowledge in an analytical way. Test-taking skills will help you do this efficiently.

The previous chapter offered study strategies to help you prepare for your tests. Preparation is 90 percent of the battle. The more prepared you are, the more relaxed you are and the less anxious you feel. The more relaxed you are during a test, the better you perform. While preparation is key, you still have to execute on test day. This chapter is all about capitalizing on what you've achieved from practicing good time management and effective study and classroom skills. The strategies presented here will help to instill a sense of confidence, no matter what type of exam situation you find yourself in.

Ignore the Pretest Chatter

I usually recommend that students arrive in class a few minutes early to get settled and be ready to go when the professor begins. The only day I do *not* recommend getting to class early is on test day. Test day is the day when many of your classmates will get to class early to "review." There is actually very little reviewing going on in the classroom right before a test. For the most part, there's only chatter and a whole lot of exaggerating going on.

When I give tests in my class, I notice there are two usual suspects that emerge prior to every test. One is a student who tells classmates how *little* he studied, and the second is a student who tells classmates how *much* he studied. These two students always talk louder than everyone else and ultimately make their fellow classmates very nervous. When I returned to school as a freshman, I'd go to class early on test day and quietly observe the various interactions around me. Guess what I saw. You guessed it, the same two suspects. As a professor, I studied the results of the two suspects in hopes of relaxing my future students. If I heard a student say to classmates on test day anything resembling "I didn't study much," I separated their tests after they handed them in. Grades of those tests were both low scoring and high scoring—high scoring to the point that it was clear these individuals studied a great deal. Maybe these high-scoring students believed they could never study enough. Or perhaps some were even lying when they announced, "I didn't study much." I don't know. Either way, there's nothing gained by listening to these students. The second type of student that could make others nervous would say something along the lines of, "I studied ten hours yesterday for the exam!" Since you're familiar with my time-management theories, you know that this marathon approach to studying is terrible. Not only do I not believe this student, but if she did in fact study for ten hours, her study session was ineffective and most of the time was wasted.

Do you see why I don't want you to be around such negativity before the test? No good can possibly come from it. Get to class a minute or two early, find your seat, and relax. Take a moment to breathe, and don't look at any notes. Don't let these students distract you, destroy your confidence, or lessen your focus. You have done your studying. You're prepared. It's time to be confident.

Start with Your Strongest Section

I've watched many students take many tests, and for some reason, most insist on starting with question #1. We are often taught to start at the beginning, but this is not necessarily the best way to take a test. Before starting to answer questions, scan the test first, and then start the test at the section in which you are strongest.

Starting the test where you choose has many benefits. First of all, momentum is powerful in test-taking. A great start sets you up for a great finish. You build momentum, and you build confidence. The positive effect of momentum cannot be understated in test-taking.

The second benefit is related to timing. Your strongest section is also probably the section you'll move fastest in. By starting with your strongest section, you're likely to get ahead in your timing a little bit. This has a relaxing effect during a test, which will enhance your effectiveness on the remaining portions. Getting ahead creates more time for the sections you may find more challenging.

> Scan the test. Start with your strongest section.

Employ a Timing Strategy

The most powerful tactic you can employ during test-taking is a timing strategy. Assuming you have taken the SAT or ACT, you know that timing can make or break you. That will be true with any test. However, your strategy during college tests will be far simpler. In your test, you're seeking a strategy that keeps you on track, eliminates wasted time, and does not create another task. This is the goal of any time-management strategy.

Your professor may recommend that you "watch the clock" during the test, though that's not enough of a strategy. In fairness, it's not the professor's job to create a timing strategy for you. A timing strategy should be customized, and the professor's job is to teach the class as a whole. A theme we've returned to again and again in this book is that your college will deliver information and you must subsequently customize it. That's what a strategic student does.

There are two general categories of tests: (1) essay or short-answer tests and (2) problem-solving tests. For both categories, the following general strategies work for most students.

Essay or Short-Answer Tests

Prior to the test, you'll know how many questions are on it, assuming you've seen a practice test and/or the professor has provided this information. Before test day, ask the professor what length of answer she's seeking. Now comes some elementary division: divide the test time by the number of questions to give you your time allotment per question. *Do this the night before, not during the test.* Wear a digital watch during the exam and glance at it as you start every question, noting when you "should" finish that question. Do the easy questions first, and you'll get ahead.

Problem-Solving Tests

Math and science classes tend to have more problems and differing sections. Timing each question is too much work during a test. I've found that setting a time per page works well. Divide the class time by the number of pages, and mark your time at the start and finish of each page. If you're taking a computer-based test, determine how much time you want to spend on a set of problems (for example, check the clock every five or ten problems). Remember, you should still start with your strongest section to gain momentum.

Avoid Misreading a Question

You know about the value of timing yourself and moving through a test at a consistent pace. It's also important to resist answering a question instantly; wait until you've asked yourself: *"What concept(s) is this question testing?"*

The risk of not asking yourself this question is that you may move forward with the wrong knowledge set (for example, the wrong equation to use) and assumptions and answer the question incorrectly.

High-school exams often test you on facts—largely material you memorized. In college, you're being tested on concepts and how to apply them. By asking yourself, "What concept(s) is this question testing?" you'll first identify what concepts you're being asked about; second, you'll access what you've learned about these concepts; and third, you'll apply that knowledge to the answer. Doing so takes only a second or two but pays off by eliminating those questions that you'll answer incorrectly because you "misread" the question.

Give Concise Answers

At some point in your college career, you'll probably be given a short-answer or essay test. I've noticed a trend while grading these tests—I call it "over-answering." Many students think a good technique for these types of tests is to write and keep writing in the hopes that they stumble upon what they think the professor is looking for. This is a misconception. Providing the right answer and surrounding it with five wrong answers is not a good strategy.

Over-answering is the conversational equivalent of rambling—nothing screams "I don't know!" like rambling. In other words, you're communicating to the individual reading the exam that you don't have a clue. This is not the message to send to that person with the red pen. Put yourself in the grader's shoes.

What does that person want to hear? If you don't know, guess, but don't ramble. You can also ask your professor prior to the test what he or she believes is an ideal answer length. Your professor has many tests to grade and is looking for accurate, concise answers.

Be Disciplined: Don't Linger over One Question

Test-taking requires focus and discipline. The focus part of the equation makes sense to students, but often they're confused by test-taking discipline. It takes discipline to do the extras on test day. For example, it takes discipline to incorporate timing principles. Your professor will not require you to jot down times and track your progress, but a disciplined student will do it anyway and she will be rewarded by her high scores.

I recommend to students that they skip questions they don't know immediately, move on, and come back later. The quicker you move on, the better. Students sometimes resist this advice because it may feel like quitting. If you're reading this book, you are a proactive person who likes finishing things you've started. That's a great quality to have, but it can work against you while test-taking. It takes discipline to quickly acknowledge you don't know something and move on. Grinding out an answer will consume too much time. Another benefit of moving on is that there's a great chance another problem or question will jar loose the answer that wasn't coming earlier. Sometimes you may even find the answer somewhere else on the test.

Early Finishers Don't Do Better

When I first started giving tests in my class, I noticed there were always a few students who completed tests very early. These students acted smooth in their departure, with a confident walk to the door. I also noticed that some other students' eyes would open wide in shock. On separate occasions, a few students mentioned to me that they felt stressed when some of their classmates left early while they still had so much more to do. Their assumption was that these students really knew their stuff. That assumption is usually false.

I completely understand why seeing a classmate depart a test early could cause stress, so I conducted a little experiment. Over the course of a semester, every time I gave a test or quiz, I marked the first three tests handed in. Out of all the tests I gave that semester, not one time did any of the first three finishers get an A. Not once. My conclusion is that first finishers are not departing because they did so well; they're departing because they don't have much more to give so they just leave.

By the way, the final finishers were never the top scorers either—you know, the students who are hustling in the last seconds while the professor begs them to hand in the test. They don't do well either. The A's were usually the students who thoughtfully moved through the test at an appropriate pace and finished right on time.

I had this knowledge when I returned to school yet still felt a small jolt of anxiety when that first test was handed in with lots of time left on the clock. I then quickly reminded myself of my experiment as a professor and moved on at an efficient pace. My experiment should serve as nice reminder to you to *relax* when that first test is handed in. It's usually meaningless.

Essay Questions: Start with an Outline

The tests I gave in my class were composed of all essay questions. One of my very best students, Evan, used to put a blank piece of paper by his side and make notes on it throughout the test. I asked Evan to see his notes, and I found that he was making very short outlines (three to five bullet points) for his test answers. On subsequent tests, I watched the other students; the vast majority of them would just start writing answers without first jotting down any notes. I suggested to the class that an outline would help to streamline thoughts, save time, and eliminate rambling. Many took my recommendation, and guess what happened. The class average of my test grades rose significantly.

Another benefit to outlining can come in the form of partial credit. If you are rushing to finish a test and don't have time to write your fully developed essay, jot down your outline and get partial credit. I gave a student almost full credit to a question when she jotted down an outline at the end of the test because I could tell she knew the answer and just ran out of time. By the way, I also pulled her aside and coached her on employing a timing strategy; she never had to throw down an outline again. Combining a timing strategy with outlining on an essay test is a recipe for success.

Math and Science Exams: Show Your Work

Always show your work through each step of a test problem. Many times, professors want to understand your approach to answering the question and will give you partial credit if you understand the general steps to get to a solution but still calculate the wrong answer. The process is worth more than the final answer.

Show all of your work. If you don't show your work, the only criteria your professor can grade you on is your final answer. Even if your approach to solving the problem is 100 percent correct, if you made a math error, you may not get any credit. However, if you show your work you may get most of the credit even if you made a math error somewhere along the process. Showing your work also helps you organize your problem-solving method similarly to an outline for an essay.

Make sure that you make it clear which equations you are using to solve the problem before inputting any actual numbers. One student I interviewed, Mark, reported, "I always made sure to define each variable explicitly ($x=10$, $y=15$, etc.) so that it was easy for the professor to understand which equations I was using to solve the problem." This is a much better approach than just writing numbers down on a page with no context of the actual equations. Mark was putting himself in the shoes of his professor. I am sure the professor appreciated it. By the way, Mark was an A-student in the school of engineering.

Multiple-Choice Exams

In most multiple-choice exams, there is one answer that is clearly incorrect and can be eliminated. If you don't know the answer to the question utilizing the methods previously discussed, it is helpful to eliminate incorrect answers before determining the right answer. It helps cut down on your options and increases your chance of guessing right if you need to guess. It also allows you to narrow the problem down quickly and move on to other questions. One student of mine told me that she would eliminate incorrect answers and then come back later and spend more time trying to figure out the right answer before the end of the test. What a great strategy!

Summary

Veterans understand that success on the battlefield truly begins with preparation. The more demanding you are in training, the greater the likelihood you will execute successfully in real battle. The ultimate weapon in acing tests is obviously preparation. This book is mostly about preparation, but at the end of the day, you still have to execute a great test. Employing the test-taking skills described in this chapter coupled with a disciplined mind-set will help you capitalize on your prior preparation efforts (time-management, studying, and classroom skills). Knowing that you prepared properly for the test and paced yourself efficiently during the test is a great feeling—and a tremendous confidence booster because with each test, your skills become honed, your instincts become sounder, and your belief in strategizing is strengthened.

Chapter 8

Paper-Writing Skills: Strategies for an A Paper

Write your first draft with your heart.
Rewrite with your head.
—From the Movie *Finding Forrester*

Paper writing is one of the most daunting tasks in college. Veterans especially struggle with writing. I believe this is because while the military can be academically demanding, there is very little writing necessary until you reach a high level of seniority. As a result, oftentimes, veterans have not written a paper in many years. There is no avoiding writing in college (or life); it is an essential skill. It also requires mastering important skills because papers are worth so much credit; they can really make or break your grade in a class. I assigned one paper in the class I taught, and it was worth 25 percent of the final grade. I've often heard students share sentiments such as, "I'm a good writer" or "I'm not a good writer," as if their writing ability had been defined at birth. Those feelings stem in part from the quality of writing training the students received in high school and earlier. I received no writing training in the military, and the chances are unless you were a journalist, neither did you. Like so many other skills, writing can be cultivated with guidance and practice. College paper writing does not require you to be the next Shakespeare or even J. K. Rowling. An A paper is well within the reach of every student because most college writing (creative writing excluded) is built around researching, presenting arguments, and developing and sharing your own perspectives.

There are many excellent books and online resources available on how to write effective papers, and I encourage you to explore some of them. While this chapter won't teach you how to compose the perfect paper, it will discuss some of the basic strategies and skills surrounding paper preparation.

Paper Writing Do's and Don'ts

On the first day of class, you'll most likely receive a syllabus that will include the paper assignments for the semester. Many students will ignore this information because the due dates seem far away. *The key to writing an A paper lies in starting early and employing resources around you.* Marking the due date on your calendar is the first step, but you'll also want to set up a writing schedule that keeps you on track. Here's my general philosophy on paper writing:

- Multiple, short writing sessions produce a high-quality paper.
- Long writing sessions produce a low-quality paper.

Sound familiar? Paper writing is like studying—marathon studying is much less effective than short-interval studying. Similarly, writing turns out sloppy if you try to do it all at once. Yet when you schedule writing as a process of intervals over time, the results are dramatically better. This is why you have to personalize a writing plan that suits your schedule. Establishing daily and weekly objectives—what you intend to achieve—will help get your paper written on time and any other deliverables your professor may expect from you accomplished.

Scheduling writing during weeks you don't have any other tests or commitments ensures that you have adequate, consecutive blocks of time to make progress on your paper. Your professor may have one key date, and that is the date you turn in the paper.

You must assign yourself weekly objectives to break up the paper-writing process.

> The key to writing a great paper is starting it early and engaging supporting resources.

Another benefit to starting early is that it gets you thinking about the topic. Valuable thought-development sessions can occur at the gym, on the bus, or even walking across campus. "Incubation" time is essential to developing thoughts; if you wait until the last minute, you end up just typing, not communicating. If you procrastinate too long before starting a paper, you'll feel rushed, your thoughts will be underdeveloped, and your grade will reflect that.

Length of Papers

Most professors give a page range for an assigned paper. For example, I assigned a paper that was to run three to five pages. There's absolutely no correlation between longer papers and higher grades. Many students believe that the more they write, the more likely they are to get a higher grade. A great paper is a great paper regardless of length. Likewise, when I was reading a lousy paper, I never thought, *Wow, this paper is really bad; I hope it goes on longer.* Sometimes, less is more. If you need five pages to make your point, by all means, use it, but if you can do it in three, that's fine, too. Never go over the required maximum; it's there for a reason. Grading papers is the most time-consuming task professors do, so don't waste their time. They'll appreciate that.

Mark Twain Understood the Power of Brevity

The legendary author wrote in a letter to a friend that he "would like to have written a shorter letter but didn't have the time." Mark Twain understood that delivering a thoughtful and purposeful message in a concise format is much more difficult to do than to continue writing for many pages. A college professor will likely be very impressed with your ability to communicate a concise, thoughtful, and well-written point. People who ramble usually don't have much to say.

The Writing Process

Writing a paper occurs in stages. Before you even begin writing, a number of important steps should be taken first. Many students think they're not making progress until they actually start writing. This is far from the truth. You're setting yourself up for an A paper, not just a completed paper. Below is a five-point plan for writing a winning paper, from selecting your topic to proofreading your final version.

1. Select a Topic

Early into the semester, schedule a short meeting with your professor during his or her office hours. Present a written topic and a few general ideas in regards to developing your main theme. Not only will your professor be impressed that you're starting so early (that alone is a victory), but the meeting could potentially save you from spending weeks on a topic your professor thinks is not a good one. During the meeting, your professor will help you refine your objectives and possible structure. You can even ask your professor about particular writing or research resources that would be useful.

2. Begin Your Research

Researching is so easy that your biggest problem is going to be narrowing down the sea of information to a few carefully chosen resources. Research does *not* constitute Googling information and calling it a day. Professors are also keenly aware of Wikipedia and its content. Wikipedia is a fine resource for some general ideas, but keep in mind who authors wikis—*anybody*. Professors prefer professional sources of research, such as journals, magazine articles, and books. Seek out sources of research in which the author is an expert in his or her field. Researching in general means reading other people's thoughts as a means to developing your own. Read, take notes, and think about which direction to head in.

3. Brainstorm

You haven't written one page yet you've completed a great deal toward your paper thus far. I recommend brainstorming using a word-processing or spreadsheet document. Here's one technique a student, Erik, showed me that I thought was brilliant. Erik used text boxes in a Microsoft Word file to jot down ideas in the form of subject categories and subcategories from his research. By placing ideas in boxes, Erik could move them around into different outline progressions until one suited him, kind of like if they were magnets on a board. With this method, you don't have to think or plan in a linear format yet (such as an outline), which can hinder creativity. Let's look at a simple example. For his film history class, Erik is going to argue that Martin Scorsese is the most influential filmmaker ever. His initial brainstorm is shown in figure 8.1.

Erik's Paper Brainstorm

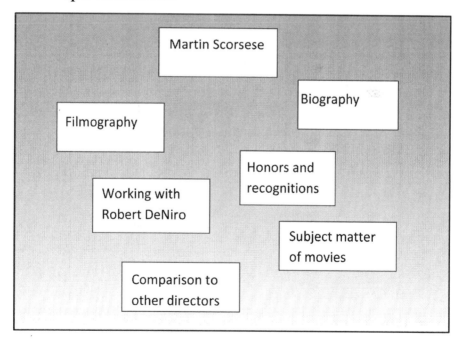

Figure 8.1. Erik's ideas are in no particular order just yet. He can do that later.

Obviously, Erik's thoughts are not fully flushed out, but now he can move them around, add, or eliminate material until his main themes and arguments start to emerge.

4. Create an Outline

You've settled on a flow via your brainstorming exercise, and now it's time to elaborate on your thoughts. Use your brainstorm to convert your ideas into a linear outline in a word-processing program, such as Microsoft Word or Google Docs. A linear outline will put your ideas into the order that the paper will read, and you can elaborate on each theme that you want to communicate. Now is also the time to decide on your primary sources of research. I recommend using multiple sources of research to fully develop your arguments and message. As a general rule, I recommend using at least one resource for every page of the paper. For example, a five-page paper should utilize at least five resources.

When your outline is complete, make another appointment with your professor to discuss your outline. Tell her what you've discovered in your research and how it's affecting your objectives. Her feedback will either support you in the direction you're taking or will get you to think about other perspectives. Professors typically love to offer guidance when asked, but few students take the initiative to ask. Professors have a wealth of experience and expertise, and you can benefit greatly by tapping into this.

Here's a strategy question: if your professor has helped guide you in your paper writing and you implemented the changes she suggested, is she more likely to give you a high grade or a low grade? The answer should be obvious.

5. Write the Paper

Now it's time to state your topic and elaborate on your supporting ideas. Using your detailed outline, which lists the sources you'll cite, you'll be surprised how easily this step unfolds. Don't aim for perfection on your first draft. It's much more important just to get the information down. When the paper seems fairly complete, put it away. After a day or two, review it carefully, looking to tighten your sentences, embellish or delete as needed, and fix typos.

Seek a reader for your paper. This could be your teaching assistant (TA), a graduate student, or even another well-respected student (perhaps one majoring in writing). Ask this person for feedback. Utilizing an outside reader will help you see problems that you have missed because you are so close to the paper that it's difficult to be completely objective.

The main theme of this paper-writing methodology is you are including your professor in the process. Professors want to help you, and this is why they have office hours. None of these steps will be required, but the likelihood of you scoring a high grade is significantly higher than if you went at it as a solo pursuit. From a time-management perspective, this didn't take you any more time. Writing requires multiple steps to produce a high-quality paper, and the actual writing and editing of the paper is the final step.

If English is your second language, the difficulty of writing is magnified; however, you can overcome this obstacle. Most campuses have a center for international students and often have writing workshops as part of their services. It is worth a call or visit to the center to utilize this resource. The five writing steps I delineated above will work for international students too; however, when English is your second language, the editing process will take a slightly longer amount of time and you can benefit from utilizing multiple reviewers of your paper.

Campus Resources

There are so many helpful resources on campus when it comes to writing. My favorites are the English and writing departments. Most writing departments host open proofreading hours or even offer tutoring appointments available to all students at the school. Some schools will even require graduate students to work a few hours a week in this capacity. This is an amazing opportunity to get some expert eyes on your paper.

Little known fact: you don't need to be an English or writing major to utilize those resource centers. I had a political science student who loved to walk over to the English department and have a tutor look at his papers. Once again, though, no one will tell you about these resources, nor will they seek you out. I recommend that you finish your paper a week or two early and seek out one of these departments. In other words, don't swing by the department the day before your paper is due.

Writing about your military experience

I read recently that student veterans rarely write about their military experience in college. A few students I interviewed said they were not comfortable doing so. Others said they feared their professor could be "antimilitary" and thus it could affect their class performance. I would never advocate writing about your experience if you are not comfortable doing so. I would like to share that I've read papers by veterans who did share their experiences, and they were thoughtful and wise. Writing professors I spoke with told me that they found that the depth and perspective of veterans added a tremendous value to their classes.

Another positive side effect is that writing about your personal experience serves as a powerful medium to educate professors about the overall military experience. This certainly isn't your responsibility, but it does make me a proud teacher and veteran when another professor who wasn't in the military says to me, "I learned so much from [name] and his or her military experience." Most importantly, I believe writing about your experience also helps you make the connection between all you learned in the military with what you are learning in school. The goal of being a student veteran is to build upon your military experience. With that being said, please consider incorporating your military career into your writing—you may find the experience to be positive.

Summary

There are many different types of papers written in college. The basic steps in this chapter will get you pointed in the right direction and are applicable to almost all research-style papers. The key ingredient to success presented in this chapter is that you are employing the professor as a partner (this helps with getting to know your professor too). As soon as you get your writing assignment, begin to plan your schedule to ensure you'll have adequate time to complete all the steps needed to produce a great paper. Many fine books and online resources exist on the topic of writing, and I encourage you to explore those for specific techniques to help improve your skills. Additionally, your campus will have writing experts in the English department. I encourage you to seek them out. However, I'm confident that if you set out by heeding the suggestions presented in this chapter, you'll be on your way to becoming a confident and effective writer who will score high grades on paper assignments.

PART THREE

Tools to Enhance Well-Being and Learning

Chapter 9

Managing Stress

If you ask me what is the single most important key to longevity,
I would have to say it is avoiding worry, stress and tension.
And if you didn't ask me, I'd still have to say it.
—George Burns

College life is very demanding, and transitioning from the military can magnify the stress that is already inherent to academics. The good news that I tell all college-bound veterans is what you have done in the military is much more difficult than what you are about to do. This seems to relax them a bit. One of the biggest adjustments that causes stress to veterans is the perception that college is a very selfish environment. Veterans have come from a very selfless environment. You do very little solo in the military; it is the ultimate team pursuit. Adjusting to this solo mission, a hectic schedule, and managing a heavy workload are some of the pressures that can take a toll on students, leading to stress. The approaches discussed in this book—applying a strategic mind-set, managing your time efficiently, and developing your academic skills—are ultimately designed to help reduce stress and thus maximize your well-being and performance throughout your college career.

The Stress Cycle

We tend to think of stress as a bad thing, but some stress is actually good. It can be a motivating and focusing force. Too much stress though can impair our health, learning abilities, and performance. Anyone who has undergone any type of weapons training already understands the stress cycle. When military members are preparing to fire a weapon with live ordnance, they are taught to stay relaxed. Relaxation allows the shooter to remain flexible and adjust to any changes in the environment. It seems contradictory to teach relaxation while harnessing a combat skill, but it is done for a reason.

When an infantry marine, for example, has to conduct an amphibious assault, he needs to be relaxed enough to retain accuracy and yet aggressive enough to advance forward. It is understandable that he can become overly stressed, causing greater tension, and now his shooting accuracy is further degraded. He's caught in a stress cycle and has to break it to accomplish the mission. This exact same cycle occurs in academics.

When I see students "stressing out," I instantly assume they are not going to do well—just like in weapons training, they won't hit the target until they relax. It's a vicious cycle because the student's stress causes them to perform poorly in school and then performing poorly causes more stress and they end up doing even worse. Time management is the cycle breaker. I find it ironic that the seemingly not-so-laid-back habit of tracking time makes you a more relaxed student and person, but it does. In addition to helping you relax more, managing stress will get you higher grades. When you're under stress, your body releases hormones. These hormones are involved in various bodily functions, including neurotransmission. When stress hormones interfere with neurotransmission, intellectual functions, such as memory, concentration, and other cognitive activities, are impaired. Did you ever get a test back and notice something you "totally knew the answer to" and wonder why you got it wrong? That very well may have been the result of stress.

College is stressful, and no combination of habits will completely eliminate it. Moreover, there will always be stressful situations you have no control over, like an accident or illness of a loved one. You can, however, keep stress in check by practicing healthy lifestyle habits. Remember, some stress is good and can be your friend. This is the stress that will drive you to get out of bed early in the morning to finish your biology lab assignment (most of us probably don't want to get out of bed to do a biology lab assignment). Just being aware of stress and how it works will motivate you to deploy the stress-fighting skills discussed in this book.

Get Enough Exercise, Sleep, and Good Nutrition

Trying to educate college students about nutrition is like trying to teach a fish to ride a bike. They just don't seem to go together. But veterans seem to understand the value of physical fitness more than traditional students. My goal is not to teach you about nutrition or exercise—I'm not an expert, and there are plenty of awesome books on these subjects. But I would like to share a few observations regarding the relationship between physical/mental health and academics. Physical health and mental health are deeply connected, and therefore, your physical habits will greatly affect your academics.

When I was teaching NROTC at the University of Colorado, I routinely went to the recreation center to exercise. I always enjoyed seeing my fellow sailors and marines there because it gave me a chance to get to know them better outside of the classroom and office. As you know by now, I love spotting trends, and I began to notice a trend at the rec center: the students I would see at the gym were mostly my top GPA scorers. I wondered why that was, so I began to incorporate a question about exercise and nutrition into my student interviews.

My interviews told me that about 75 percent of my A students exercised routinely and "tried" to eat healthy.

Those who exercised regularly and slept reasonably well usually performed better academically. I am not implying that this is a causal relationship. In other words, I don't believe that good grades are the result of exercise, but what I can say confidently is that healthy physical habits are powerful weapons for defeating stress. Therefore, if stress is the enemy of academic success and exercise suppresses stress, then logic dictates that healthy physical habits do in fact make you a better student. PT breaks the stress cycle; it's a classic naval strategy of interrupting and breaking up the supply chain!

I'd also like to share another observation: most of my struggling students did not exercise routinely. The most cited reason: "I just don't have time." I find it extremely interesting that my A students had time to exercise yet my struggling students did not. I hope by now you're seeing that the habits of successful individuals are usually not isolated to one area of their life. My academically successful students were also very "together" in their personal lives. For example, my A students rarely had issues with personal finance. My struggling students often did. My A students took care of their mind and body; even their social lives were better. My conclusion is that the habits and mind-set utilized to defeat stress in your academic life are the very same habits that will help you succeed in the rest of your life.

My advice is to schedule your workouts, set your nutritional and sleep goals, and make note of how you feel. You may even consider keeping an exercise journal, as you are now aware of the powers of tracking. If you miss a workout, it's no big deal—just get back on schedule. If you have a bad night's sleep, try to get a good one the next night. However, if you find yourself canceling workouts because you consistently "don't have time," I recommend you use that as a warning; I bet other areas of your life are suffering as well. It might help to brush up on your time-management skills to help break this cycle.

> Healthy physical habits relieve stress. Less stress makes you a better student.

Spirituality as a Source of Stress Relief

Spirituality is another positive source of mental and physical health for many students. Spirituality is personally defined. For some, it may mean going to a weekly religious service, while for others, it may mean a Saturday afternoon yoga class. I had one student who rode the same mountain bike trail every Sunday and told me that she found peace in the weekly ride. The source of spirituality does not matter too much. What does matter is that my students, who felt a spiritual calling reported that they found peace, balance, and stress relief by embracing their spirituality and that helped them focus better on academics.

Find Mentors

Mentors are essential to success. Mentors are people you look up to and would like to emulate. They are people who have expertise and can share wisdom with you. Mentors can be advisors and professors, but mentors should also include peers. Peers are often closer in age and circumstance to you than your professors or advisors. Ever notice in the military that generals don't mentor privates? There is just too much experience and rank separation between the two. I made it to O-4 in the navy, and during my decade of service, I never had a single conversation with an admiral, but I had some wonderful E-8 and O-5 mentors. You know who the best mentor for a private is? Someone who was a private a year or two ago, someone who remembers clearly what it was like, like it was yesterday. An E-5, for example, is much closer to the challenges that an E-2 is facing and therefore is a powerful mentor. Senior leadership is still a wonderful source of mentorship, but if it is used alone, your mentor network will be incomplete and thus weaker than if it includes peer mentors.

Notice I am not advocating for a single mentor; instead, I recommend developing a mentor network. The reason I believe in a mentor network so strongly is because relying on one-on-one mentorship only is usually doomed to fail. It requires a perfect match between mentor and mentee, and that is not a reasonable expectation in college or life. One person cannot be an expert on all the areas of your life, nor is that person always available. In my life, I have many mentors. I have teaching mentors, business mentors, and even life mentors. I don't necessarily declare each person with the title of "mentor," but I do often rely on them for guidance. In college, I recommend you start building your mentor network early. Seek professors and staff members but also peers. In other words, build a team. Teams create a bigger impact on the world than individuals.

So what does a college peer mentor do? A peer mentor is just someone who is simply further along in school or a career than you are. He or she will also probably have something in common with you, such as your course of study, sports team, or club affiliation. The reason mentors are so valuable in college is because they've done exactly what you're trying to do. They can provide real-time guidance on issues that advisors might fall short on. Questions like, "How is that professor?" or "Do you recommend that course?" are best suited to fellow students, not advisors or professors.

A relationship with a mentor doesn't have to be formal, although some veterans departments will have a formal program. If there is a program, I recommend you use it, but if not, don't worry—you can benefit from a mentor without any formalities. A nice combination of mentors should include student veterans in your major, alumni who have progressed in your chosen career, and, of course, advisors who are dedicated to your success. As a veteran, you are part of an amazing community. Veterans have each other's back and always will. Camaraderie doesn't end because we left the service, and that is an incredible life advantage. But here is the deal. For mentor networks to work, you have to give mentorship and not just receive it.

> Student mentors provide advice and guidance that others can't.

Don't Be a Study Hermit

I am an advocate for blowing off steam. Whatever you enjoy doing for fun, don't stop. It's part of the college experience. If it relieves stress, then I am for it.

I've included this section to highlight that nowhere in my strategic advice do I advocate becoming a hermit. The time-management and study strategies are all designed to maximize learning in minimal time. You don't have to miss a single party, football game, or any other social event in college if you're a good time manager. In fact, I want you to socialize because it creates a more balanced mind-set than if you were locked away in a study room feeling like you were missing something fun.

If you do your work in intervals and track your progress, you don't need to miss out on anything in college. If your work is on track, then a party will actually make you a better student because you'll be enjoying your time with friends and not harboring stress about the work you haven't done yet.

Join a Team

Maintaining one's perspective helps curb stress. Students who have only academics in their lives tend to stress more about every quiz and every little point on that quiz. Eventually, they start to lose perspective and perhaps even develop tunnel vision. One way I've seen students balance their perspective is to become part of something bigger than they are, perhaps by joining a team or club or by doing volunteer work.

Like the military, life is a team sport, and most often, greatness is a team victory. I would define a team as any organization that has a mission dependent on more than just one member. Sports, a club, a band, a volunteer organization, or even a part-time job fits the bill.

While veterans organizations offer great support, I also recommend joining a team of nonveterans. I know I'm contradicting my mission for uniting student veterans, but hear me out. I recommend getting to know and understand your new classmates and their life perspectives. We all should learn from each other in college, and spending time with nonmilitary classmates will help ease your own transition. Furthermore, you will be serving as a positive ambassador for all of us veterans.

There are few areas in life that we go at alone. Unfortunately, your college GPA is one of them. The college environment can be insulating and self-centered, and that can irritate veterans. But becoming part of a group effort in college has a way of reminding students that working toward a goal with others has purpose, it's part of the bigger life picture, and it provides perspective on our own lives and challenges. It can relieve stress. So consider picking something of interest and participating. Just remember to schedule your hours! (Sorry, I couldn't resist.)

Summary

This chapter is designed simply to make you aware of the role stress plays in your academic life. Stress is truly the enemy of a high GPA. You cannot alleviate all stress, but you can manage negative stress while embracing positive stress. All of your habits will contribute to stress as either a positive or negative force. Procrastinating increases stress. Managing your time decreases stress. Skipping class increases stress. Studying efficiently decreases stress. You get the point. Every decision you make in college can increase or decrease stress. Keep that in mind, and you'll make more right decisions than wrong ones, which will make you a better student. Transitioning out of the military is very difficult, the methods discussed in this book are designed to decrease academic stress and thus minimize your total stress.

Chapter 10

Harnessing the Best of Technology

Man is still the most extraordinary computer of all.
—John F. Kennedy

There's a revolution going on in colleges around the world. Three-hundred-year-old ivy-covered systems are colliding with modern networked technology. As I walked the hallways of the University of Colorado's Leeds School of Business this morning, I saw students carrying around heavy paper textbooks. That's changing, and students are now using web resources beyond their textbooks to study. I peeked into a classroom and saw most students taking notes on laptops, and a couple had tablets (mostly iPads). Some professors were writing on whiteboards with dry-erase markers. That too is changing as professors are moving toward interactive whiteboards to record their lecture notes. Students have already changed, and now universities are catching up to their population...slowly, very slowly. In other words, your school will most likely *not* be as technologically advanced as you are.

I hear many people debate the influence of technology in education, and I'm always surprised to hear it described as a "good" or "bad" thing. Technology is neither good nor evil. Similar to how money is neither good nor evil, technology is an inanimate object that can be harnessed for either. I am pro-technology and always open to hearing about innovative methods to learn and teach. My belief is that technology can be a powerful and positive force for studying and learning in college, but with this great power comes great responsibility and risks. Superheroes learn this truth when they discover their powers. Use it with integrity and caution.

Use Technology to Your Advantage

I love technology because it speaks to my theories about customizing your education. In college, information will be coming at you in a one-size-fits-all format, and technology can (and should) be used as a customization weapon. The following section describes several ways you can use technology to augment your studies.

Recorded Lectures

Some professors will record their lectures and upload them to a web-based platform like Apple's iTunes U for you to download as a podcast. The beauty of listening to a recorded lecture is that you can *pause, rewind,* or even *fast-forward.* Imagine if you could point a remote control at your professor and "pause" her until you finished writing your notes. This feature gives you that flexibility. The professor is powerful, but the student can be agile. In some ways, listening to a podcast can be even better than a live lecture because students may be reluctant to say to a professor, "Can you repeat that?" or "I don't get it." Yet with a podcast, you don't have to fear embarrassment; just hit pause or rewind. One professor I know records a few pieces of his lectures even before he presents the lecture in class because those pieces contain material that's difficult to understand. If a student listens ahead of time, he or she is poised for greater comprehension in class. What a great study aid for his students!

The disadvantages of recorded lectures are that you can't ask questions or debate and recorded lectures don't work for all class types. Classes that involve discussion and debate are not easily delivered on a podcast. But if you want to study the functions of mitochondria and you didn't quite understand the lecture, a podcast is very effective.

I also recommend that you have something visual to look at when listening to a recorded lecture. Listening to a lecture with nothing visual to follow along with is difficult. The professor's notes are great; a video (if your school records and posts lectures) is also effective. Can you imagine trying to understand organic chemistry reactions without seeing any diagrams or notes? Nearly impossible.

Online Study Aids

Who says the lecture you want to listen to has to originate from your school? Most students can't get into the Massachusetts Institute of Technology, but anyone can listen to a lecture via MIT's Open Courseware program. Another professor might deliver a lecture in a way you'll understand better. YouTube is full of videos on academic subjects that could help your studying (key word is "*could*"). The Kahn Institute is helping students learn via at-home lectures and lessons and their library of college-level courses is continuing to grow. This is a great example of customizing education to the individual student's needs. You should definitely be customizing your college education beyond simply choosing your classes.

As the classroom continues to become globalized, there are an increasing number of excellent online resources. There's also a great deal of junk on the internet. If you study from an unreliable source, there's no guarantee that the lessons are credible. Not only might you be studying erroneous or outdated information, but you'll be wasting lots of time. Talk to your professors, and ask them which sources are reliable and which ones to avoid. If nothing else, seek resources from accredited institutions, such as the MIT resource I mentioned.

There are also a few "social learning" websites that provide notes, past exams, problem sets, and study guides. Koofers and Course Hero are examples. If used responsibly, they can be very helpful. If you like a set of notes on Koofers, that's great...but check the material for validity by cross-referencing facts with proven sources, such as a textbook or university-sourced information;

doing so will make for a great study session. Cut and paste the material into your notes for maximum effectiveness.

Digital Notes

I previously discussed digital note-taking in chapter 5, but what I didn't mention is where to store those notes. I recommend web-based storage, such as Google Docs or Dropbox. If you carry around your laptop, storing your notes on your hard drive is fine because the notes will be accessible—just make sure you're backing up your notes to a web-based storage site, such as Dropbox or Google Drive (there are several more options, many of which are *free*) or an external hard drive. Web-based storage is the best because of the constant accessibility it provides. You never know when a pocket of study time may present itself, and of course, you won't want to always carry around your laptop or books. Access your notes from an iPad or mobile phone and watch those pockets of study time add up.

Online Classes

Online classes have dramatically increased in popularity, and I believe they will continue to as technology improves. In fact, you can now obtain an entire college degree online from great universities. I've been asked many times if I find online degrees to be credible. I say it depends on the school and the class. I still prefer in-person sessions augmented with online learning. There is too much lost by not interacting in person with fellow classmates and instructors. We still live in a world that requires people skills, and learning to work in teams, giving presentations to a live audience, brainstorming, listening to others, and debating is huge part of collegiate learning. With that being said, for some people, online degrees provide an educational option that otherwise wouldn't be available to them because of geographic distance or work schedules. Therefore, I don't discredit online degrees; I simply prefer traditional degrees (blended with technology) if it is an option for you.

While I prefer traditional (in class) degrees, I do believe individual online classes can fit nicely into your degree program. Certain classes can be very effectively delivered online, and your school will probably offer this option. Online classes are great options to use in moderation. But before choosing to take one, I recommend you consider what types of classes are effectively delivered online and subsequently consider the advantages and disadvantages of an online class. Once you've conducted this analysis, I believe you can now make an informed decision whether or not to enroll in an online class.

Not all class types are effectively delivered online. Classes that require discussion and debate and/or in-person collaborative teamwork are not as effectively delivered online. This sort of human interaction, which is professor-led and classmate fueled, is an extremely valuable learning method and cannot be fully replicated on a computer. Therefore, if possible, I would not consider taking classes, such as political science, ethics, leadership, or history (to name a few), in the online format.

Which classes are good choices for online delivery? Subjects that require minimal or no interpretation and therefore require little live discussion and/or teamwork can be effectively delivered online. Examples of such classes include financial accounting and sciences that don't require a laboratory session, such as anatomy or physiology. Computer science and mathematical classes can also be effectively delivered online, especially if they include problems and exercises that measure your learning progress and therefore alert you to review a concept if you haven't mastered it yet.

There are many advantages to online classes. The most obvious advantage is the flexibility of not having a scheduled class time. You can study where you want when you want; an online class will never present a scheduling conflict. A second advantage is that you decide the pace in which you complete the class sessions. Of course, you will have due dates and deadlines, but the actual class lessons can be paced at your discretion. No more feeling left behind in class; not to mention you can pause or rewind whenever you choose! Haven't you always wanted to "pause" or "rewind" a teacher in the middle of class? A final advantage is the increase in class options available to you. With online learning, you are not limited by your physical location or school; you may be able to complete an online class for credit at another university if that class is not available at your school. There are also many disadvantages to online classes. They are impersonal, and classroom discussion cannot be replicated. A second disadvantage is that non-verbal communication is mostly one-way, meaning the professor is unable to read the body language of the class. Professors in a classroom can sense whether or not the students are responsive and adjust the lesson accordingly. This agility is lost online. A final disadvantage is the minimal ability to learn from your classmates. Collegiate learning is in large part a live exchange of ideas between your professor, you, and your classmates. With online classes, teamwork and real-time discussion are greatly limited.

Many educators believe that online classes are often favored by less-motivated students who are too lazy to go to class. I believe this to be a misconception and that it takes a very motivated student to learn successfully via an online class. If you take an online class, you have to be disciplined enough to follow a reasonably paced schedule because you do not attend weekly classes nor is a professor assessing your learning via in-class dialogue. You must self-assess, and that takes honesty and discipline. Time-management skills are perhaps even more important to utilize in online courses.

In summary, I have no problem with students taking online classes, but I recommend they do so in moderation (no more than one or two per semester) and only for the right type of classes (ones that require minimal dialogue and in-person collaboration). Technology will continue to progress, and professors will develop more effective methods of teaching online. But for now, I still favor live class sessions for the majority of your education (supplemented with technology). I do reserve the right to change my mind though because technology is getting better and better.

Online Classes Are Different from Virtual Classes

Virtual classes take place online; however, they are viewed live at a specified time, much like a traditional classroom. They are not necessarily recorded, and the pace is still determined by the professor. Many classes have a medium for asking questions via voice or instant message. The advantage of virtual classes is you can take them from any location that has Internet access. They differ from online classes because online classes are self-paced and self-study. Ensure you understand the difference between an online class and a virtual class before registering.

School Libraries

Wait a minute! Why would an old system like a library be in the technology chapter? Look again; libraries are not so archaic anymore. University libraries are leading the way in terms of connecting their databases to their customers. Preliminary research can often be conducted in the comfort of your dorm room via your library's online portal. Some librarians also host virtual office hours where you can ask questions via instant messaging. Once you've narrowed down your research options, you are now prepared to visit the library with a more focused list of potential research sources. Some universities are actually scanning books and making them available for online viewing! Consult with your librarian upon arrival when doing research. Librarians can be misperceived as being simply "clerks" when in fact they are invaluable resources for research, education, and mentorship.

Summary

Technology is affecting education in significant ways, both for students and teachers. Students have already embraced technology, and their encouragement is helping schools adopt technology as well. While I don't believe that technology could in any way replace the role of professors (or classmates), I do believe that technology integration can create better classroom experiences. I also believe that technology can help students arrive in class better prepared—and that benefits the learning of the entire class.

The danger of web-based study tools is that many of them lack credibility; therefore, you have to determine if the material comes from reputable sources. Furthermore, there is so much information in so many different formats that a student can drown in a sea of material. Don't forget that web-based material is for augmenting your studying and is not a primary source; your professor is still your guide. Technology is like a superpower, and like any superpower, it has the potential to cause both positive and negative outcomes. Used properly, I believe technology can empower students and teachers while fostering global learning.

Conclusion

Blame no one. Expect nothing. Do something.
—Lloyd Carr

While serving as an assistant professor of naval science and a freshman academic advisor at the University of Colorado, I became aware of a very real problem occurring in higher education: students are simply not learning the mind-set and habits needed to transition successfully from high school or the military to college. Veterans often incorrectly assume that these issues will be addressed at freshman orientation or during their first semester. Many veterans rightfully feel as though freshmen orientation doesn't address their needs. Veterans have already left home and developed a strong work ethic. They don't need a lecture on underage drinking, and yet they're asked to sit through one. Veterans are equipped to receive lessons on academic strategy, but most schools are not delivering it to them. Even if a short session is offered during orientation on transitioning to college academics, students are distracted and not prepared at that time to absorb these lessons.

I completely understand why veterans are frustrated with the current state of college orientation. Veterans already understand that strategy is taught before battle not during. I wanted to assemble a set of strategies that I could teach students *before* they got to college, which would help ensure their academic success. This may sound simplistic, but when you arrive at your college, college begins. It's game time! The semester train will start rolling with or without you. It's not your school's job to teach you how to transition or how to study. It's their job to teach you subject matter and to offer support resources.

I pondered for a long time why students struggled so much with their transition to college life before it dawned on me that the answers rested with the students I met with every day. What I needed to do was collect, organize, and test the "data" and ultimately translate it into an action plan. So I decided to examine traits of both successful and unsuccessful students. What I found was that successful students shared similar traits and unsuccessful students shared similar traits—and that success in college is not the result of brains alone; rather, it has much more to do with mind-set and habits.

I believe both mind-set and habits can be taught, practiced, and refined. I've seen students change their mind-sets and habits, and as a result, they turn academic struggles into successes. I was one of those students, and interviewing hundreds of students and subsequently testing these strategies on myself confirmed my research. I know for a fact that I'm not a brilliant person, but by using the strategies I collected, I truly accelerated my ability to learn and score higher grades.

In all sincerity, I wish someone had taken the time to teach me these lessons when I was eighteen. A major motivation for writing this book is that I hate seeing students feel defeated by their freshmen-year academics. I'm unsatisfied with college attrition among our nation's veterans. I have seen the confidence of too many students unnecessarily destroyed. I'd like to tell every student who underachieves that it's *not* because they're not smart enough. It's simply that they never learned to navigate their new academic environment. A predominant message in *The Strategic Student Veteran* is knowing that A's are within your reach if you're strategic and consistent. Yes, you absolutely have to work hard to succeed but not so hard that you're not having fun doing it.

It's not the military's job to teach you how to transition to college. They have their plate full training the next generation of warriors. Furthermore, high schools can only do so much. The reason I remind you of your high school's or college's job is because ultimately the responsibility of planning your strategy falls on your shoulders. This type of solo pursuit can be uncomfortable with veterans, but trust me, it gets easier with time and when you build your network, it's even easier.

I was a hands-on freshmen advisor, yet I felt my time was always limited in how much I could guide my students. Consequently, I learned I had to teach them to own their education. *Own your education* is my mantra and the essence of this book. It's also a requirement in college. In high school, ownership is shared between you and your teachers, counselors, coaches, and family. These people still exist in college, but they're not watching over you and you have to enlist their support. "Owning your education" means that you accept much of the responsibility that these people assumed while you were in high school. Many students really struggle with transitioning to college life, but any student can build a strategic mental framework for approaching academics. By reading this book, you've already started and you deserve credit for being proactive. This is precisely what I mean by taking ownership. Don't feel bad if all the lessons in this book don't make sense yet. My hope is that, at this point, you realize that your potential is unlimited *but* only if it is properly harnessed.

If you are currently a college student and you are reading this book after struggling a bit in college, I am glad you are here. You are picking yourself up, dusting yourself off, and getting back in the fight. We are all entitled to second chances, and everybody loves a comeback story. If you are job seeking or applying to graduate school, your hill is steeper, but your goals are very much still achievable. Break the cycle, and show the world your upward trend. Trust me, someone will believe in you.

Ever watch the TV show *The Biggest Loser*? On the show, overweight people are struggling to lose pounds, but more important, they are trying to get a healthy mental and physical life back. Success for these contestants is defined as obtaining a healthy weight (and potentially winning one million dollars). What is the first thing their trainers do with the contestants? Convince them of the need to "track." The contestants all track their calories throughout the day—the calories they take in and the calories they burn. Tracking is a key to success. One of the smartest habits you can adopt in college is to track your study hours because it's often too late to pull up your grades by the time you receive your grades. Estimating and tracking your study time will guide you toward balance and success in college. It takes a minute a day and saves you an invaluable amount of time, stress, and heartache. Working hard is great; working balanced and smart is much better.

Universities are designed to deliver information. In a one-size-fits-all approach, your school will recommend how much study time you should devote to each class—without knowing your aptitude or goals. In taking ownership of your college education, you'll want to customize your study plan. Your school will also assign homework problems. You can do these assignments as given, or you can use the homework as a guideline while customizing the assignments to improve your weaker areas. I recommend customizing the assignments if they won't be graded. Customizing is gathering up all that great education that your university is delivering and personalizing it to maximize your strengths and minimize your weaknesses.

The Strategic Student Veteran is intended to plant some new seeds of thought. Whether you're an incoming freshman or a college student who's been struggling, I encourage you to reread the sections you feel will help you the most. At the very least, my hope is that you now realize your potential is unlimited *but* only if it's properly harnessed.

The reason I'm so passionate about helping students excel in college is because I know the strategies presented in this book work; after all, I interviewed hundreds of students and tested the theories on myself. I also know they'll work for you. The proper mind-set, self-reliance, and effective time-management skills level the playing field in college. Once you know that, you'll realize your goals are completely achievable. Congratulations on taking the first steps toward owning your education. Success in college is not a birthright; it's a decision. I wish you many victories throughout your academic career and beyond. I would also like to sincerely thank you for your military service. I know that your service will continue in a new form long after your graduation from college.

Other Resources

David Cass is a founder of Uvize, an education technology company dedicated to the success of student veterans. We partner with universities to deliver their online veterans center. An online veterans center is a fast mentor network that connects students with the right veteran classmate, mentor, or advisor when they need it. Uvize also delivers incoming veterans academic orientation and preparation classes in an amazing online environment. By building skills and community before school starts, we increase the success rate of veterans.

Want to get us Uvize for your school? For more information, go to *www.uvize.com.*

Acknowledgments

My most heartfelt thank-you goes to my wife, Jayme. This book would never have happened if it weren't for you. You are my advisor, editor, and best friend. I love you.

A special thanks to my parents. I never would have had the educational opportunities had it not been for you. Thank you for your endless love and support.

Thank you to the soldiers, sailors, airmen, and marines I've worked with over the years. I've learned more from than I ever could have imagined and it's been an honor to serve with you.

To David Parker, James Sanders, and Bo Bergstrom, my business partners and friends, thank you for being the creative sounding board for this project and for leading Uvize.

Thank you to my students at the University of Colorado, Boulder (especially the NROTC students). There are too many of you to list, but the lessons in this book come directly from you. Thank you to Colonel Gregory Akers, US Marine Corps (my former department professor and commanding officer), who said to me one day over coffee, "Dave, you really should write a book." Thank you for your support and mentorship; it was an honor to work for you.

Thank you to my editor, Jody Berman of Berman Editorial, for helping me through the process of becoming an author.

Thank you to Lindsay Field, of L. Field Consulting, for proofreading my writing and cleaning up my mess.

Thank you to Jason Mendelson. Our collaborative sessions, especially the early ones, truly helped me determine the strategic direction of this book and Uvize Inc. I appreciate your mentorship and friendship.

Thank you to Professor Frank Moyes at the Leeds School of Business for his inspirational teaching and continued mentorship beyond graduation.

Thank you to the Leeds School of Business at the University of Colorado, Boulder, for my time as both a student and a staff member. Your entrepreneurial spirit inspires me every day. Go Buffs!

Thank you to all the professors and advisors interviewed for this book. While there are too many to list, you know who you are. Thank you.

Thank you to my golden retriever, Nola, for sitting by my feet and snoring during all those late-night writing sessions. You are one devoted companion.

About the Author

David Cass is an adjunct professor at the Leeds School of Business at the University of Colorado in Boulder. He served previously as an undergraduate assistant professor and advisor in the university's naval science department. David is the CEO and cofounder of Uvize, Inc., an education and technology company with a focus on academic success for military veterans.

David is a former navy officer, who served as a helicopter pilot in both Operation Enduring Freedom and Operation Iraqi Freedom.

David continues service today as a lieutenant commander is the US Navy Reserves. He holds a BA in political science from Tulane University and an MBA from the University of Colorado, Boulder. David lives in Boulder with his wife, Jayme; daughters, Madelyn, and Cammie; and golden retriever, Nola.

To contact David, please go to *www.uvize.com or dave@uvize.com*